CW00543847

# Whispers of Siri: Unlocking the Magic of Apple's Enigmatic Assistant

### Robin A. Moore

Published by Robin A. Moore, 2024.

While every precaution has been taken in the preparation of this book, the publisher assumes no responsibility for errors or omissions, or for damages resulting from the use of the information contained herein.

WHISPERS OF SIRI: UNLOCKING THE MAGIC OF APPLE'S ENIGMATIC ASSISTANT

**First edition. March 17, 2024.**

Copyright © 2024 Robin A. Moore.

ISBN: 979-8224202461

Written by Robin A. Moore.

# Table of Contents

# Chapter 1: Introduction to Siri

One of the most notable advancements in recent years has been the development of virtual personal assistants, such as Apple's Siri. Siri is an intelligent assistant that uses voice recognition and natural language processing to perform a wide range of tasks, making it an invaluable tool for both personal and professional use.

Amidst these chapter, we will delve into the fascinating world of Siri, exploring its background, capabilities, and how it has revolutionized the way we interact with our devices. We will also discuss the evolution of virtual assistants, leading up to the birth of Siri and its integration into Apple's ecosystem. By the end of this chapter, you will have a solid understanding of what Siri is, how it works, and why it has become an essential part of the Apple experience.

1. 1 Understanding Siri:

Siri is an artificial intelligence-powered virtual assistant that acts as your personal guide and assistant on Apple devices. By leveraging natural language processing, Siri can understand spoken commands and queries, allowing you to interact with your iPhone, iPad, Mac, Apple Watch, and HomePod hands-free. Whether you need directions, want to set reminders, check the weather, send messages, or even book a dinner reservation, Siri is ready to assist you.

1. 2 The Evolution of Virtual Assistants:

To appreciate Siri's capabilities fully, it is essential to trace back the history of virtual assistants. The concept of a virtual assistant originated in the 1960s, but the technology needed to bring the idea to life was still in its infancy. Over the years, advancements in speech recognition, natural language understanding, and machine learning brought virtual assistants closer to reality. Siri, initially developed by the SRI International Artificial Intelligence Center, was one of the most significant breakthroughs in this field.

1. 3 Siri's Integration into Apple Ecosystem:

When Apple acquired Siri in 2010, they realized the potential it had to transform user interactions with their devices. With its first appearance on the iPhone 4S in 2011, Siri became synonymous with Apple's commitment to enhancing the user experience. Since then, Siri has expanded to other Apple products, including iPadOS, macOS, watchOS, and the smart speaker HomePod. Its cross-platform integration allows seamless communication across different devices, making Siri a truly ubiquitous virtual assistant.

1. 4 How Siri Works:

Underneath Siri's user-friendly interface lies a complex network of machine learning algorithms capable of understanding human speech patterns and context. Siri leverages the power of natural language processing, combining voice recognition, contextual cues, and a vast database of information to interpret and respond to user queries. By constantly learning from user interactions, Siri aims to provide accurate and personalized responses, improving its performance over time.

1. 5 Siri's Capabilities:

Siri's scope of capabilities is vast and ever-expanding, thanks to regular updates and Apple's integration with third-party applications. Besides general tasks like setting reminders, sending messages, and making phone calls, Siri can assist with navigation, offering real-time directions and traffic updates. Additionally, Siri can provide information on a wide range of topics, from sports scores and news updates to weather forecasts and trivia. With its integration into HomePod, Siri can even control smart home devices, playing music, adjusting thermostats, and performing various household functions.

1. 6 Customizing Siri:

To make Siri truly personalized, Apple allows users to customize certain aspects of the virtual assistant's behavior. You can customize Siri's voice to suit your preference and language accents. Moreover, you can teach Siri how to pronounce difficult names or words correctly. Siri's settings also provide options for controlling privacy, allowing users to specify what data Siri can access and use.

1. 7 Conclusion:

In conclusion, Siri has emerged as a pioneering virtual assistant that has revolutionized the way we interact with our devices. By harnessing the power of artificial intelligence, natural language processing, and machine learning,

Siri can understand and respond to complex voice commands, making our lives more convenient and efficient. As we proceed further in this book, we will explore Siri's diverse features and detailed functionalities. So, get ready to unlock the full potential of Siri and embark on an exciting journey of discovery and productivity.

# 1.1 What is Siri?

Siri is an intelligent virtual assistant developed by Apple Inc. for its iOS, iPadOS, watchOS, and macOS operating systems. It is powered by advanced artificial intelligence (AI) algorithms, which enable it to understand natural language and perform various tasks through voice commands or text input. Siri acts as your personal assistant, helping you navigate your device, search for information, set reminders, send messages, make phone calls, and much more.

In simpler terms, Siri is a voice-activated feature on Apple devices that lets you interact with your device hands-free. It utilizes sophisticated machine learning and natural language processing techniques, allowing it to understand spoken or typed commands and respond accordingly, enhancing your overall user experience. Siri serves as a technologically advanced interface, bridging the gap between humans and machines in a conversational and intuitive manner.

Among its many functionalities, Siri can perform basic tasks like setting alarms, sending messages, making appointments, and setting reminders. But it goes beyond those conventional features. Siri is also capable of providing weather forecasts, sports scores, stock prices, and even answering general knowledge questions using data from various sources on the internet.

Moreover, Siri can assist with navigation by providing directions, searching for local businesses, and estimating travel times. This comes in handy when you're planning a road trip or simply looking for the nearest coffee shop. Siri can also control smart home devices, such as lights, thermostats, and locks, making it an invaluable tool for home automation.

Besides its core functionalities, Apple constantly updates Siri to improve its capabilities and expand its integration with third-party apps. With the introduction of SiriKit, developers can integrate Siri into their apps, allowing users to perform app-specific tasks using voice commands. This opens up a world of possibilities, enabling users to accomplish tasks within different applications, all through the power of their voice.

Siri provides a seamless and intuitive user experience, allowing you to accomplish tasks faster and more efficiently. Instead of navigating through menus and typing out commands, Siri streamlines the process by acting as a virtual facilitator, translating your requests into actions executed by your device. From sending emails to playing music, Siri simplifies your digital life and brings about a new level of convenience and convenience.

In conclusion, Siri is a groundbreaking virtual assistant embedded in Apple devices, aiming to simplify the way we interact with technology. Through its integration of AI, machine learning, and natural language processing, Siri empowers users to utilize their devices in a more natural and intuitive way. By understanding spoken or typed commands, Siri enables a hands-free and efficient user experience, allowing you to accomplish tasks swiftly and seamlessly. As a beginner, this advanced assistant holds immense potential to make your Apple device an even more powerful tool in your daily life.

# 1.2 History and Development of Siri

History and Development of Siri

Apple's Siri, the intelligent virtual assistant, has become one of the most recognized and widely used voice-activated assistants in the world today. Siri was first introduced by Apple in October 2011, with its debut on the iPhone 4S. However, the journey of Siri actually began long before that, rooted in a startup project by the same name.

In 2007, Dag Kittlaus, Adam Cheyer, and Tom Gruber founded a company called Siri Inc., which initially focused on building a digital assistant that could perform a wide range of tasks by using natural language understanding and processing. Their ambition was to create a virtual assistant that could interact with users in a conversational manner, making technology more accessible and user-friendly.

Siri Inc. quickly gained attention for its impressive accomplishments in the field of artificial intelligence. The team developed an advanced software program that could interpret spoken language, execute commands, and provide responses based on the user's intent. Siri's founders garnered substantial praise, and in 2010, their company caught the eye of Apple.

Recognizing the potential of Siri, Apple bought the company in April 2010, bringing Dag Kittlaus, Adam Cheyer, and Tom Gruber onboard. Apple wanted to incorporate Siri's capabilities into its products and create a seamless user experience. The acquisition marked a remarkable turning point in voice-activated assistance technology.

Under Apple's resources and guidance, Siri underwent further development to integrate its functionality with new, cutting-edge hardware. The launch of Siri on the iPhone 4S in 2011 was a breakthrough, showcasing the power of an intelligent virtual assistant that resided in people's pockets.

By deeply integrating Siri into the iPhone's operating system, Apple enabled users to have natural, voice-driven conversations with their devices

– a previously unimaginable interaction. Siri became an integral part of iOS, marking a revolution in voice-based command systems.

Over the years, Siri has continued to evolve and expand its capabilities. Apple extended the use of Siri across its entire line of products, including iPad, Mac, Apple Watch, Apple TV, and even advanced automotive systems through Apple CarPlay. Siri is now not just present on iPhones but has become a ubiquitous feature in the Apple ecosystem.

Alongside the expansion to new devices, Apple focused on improving Siri's comprehension and accuracy for an incredible variety of tasks. Siri can now answer complex questions, set timers, send messages, play music, provide weather updates, manage appointments and reminders, control smart home devices, make reservations, book rides, and perform numerous other functions. Its seamless integration with various apps also extends its functionality considerably.

Siri's development benefited greatly from advancements in machine learning and artificial intelligence research, enabling it to continuously learn and adapt to user habits and preferences. Apple's acquisition of deep-learning startups and investments in research further propelled Siri's capability to understand natural language and provide more accurate responses.

While Siri's journey has not been entirely without pitfalls and criticism, the advancements made over time cannot be denied. Apple continually refines its virtual assistant, adding new features and improving its response time, accuracy, and overall performance, bringing it closer to human-like interactions.

In summary, Siri's history and development narrate a compelling tale of various teams' hard work and dedication towards creating a virtual assistant that helps simplify our daily lives. From its roots as an ambitious startup to its integration into Apple's widely acclaimed product lineup, Siri has come a long way, undoubtedly leaving an indelible impact on the future of virtual assistant technology.

# 1.3 Siri's Role in the Apple Ecosystem

Siri's Role in the Apple Ecosystem

Siri, the intelligent personal assistant developed by Apple, plays a vital role in enhancing the user experience within the Apple ecosystem. From its initial introduction in 2011, Siri has become an integral part of various Apple devices, including iPhones, iPads, Macs, Apple Watches, and even Apple TVs. Amidst the information in this chapter, we will delve into the diverse roles Siri fulfills within the Apple ecosystem, exploring its capabilities and how it integrates seamlessly with different Apple devices and services.

1. Siri as an Assistant

At its core, Siri serves as a digital assistant, ready to assist users in various tasks with just a voice command. From setting reminders, creating events, and managing appointments, to sending and replying to messages and emails, Siri acts as a personal secretary always within reach. With its natural language processing capabilities, Siri can understand complex queries and deliver concise and accurate responses. Users can simply ask, "Hey Siri, what's the weather like tomorrow in San Francisco?" and Siri will quickly provide the weather forecast for the specified location. Siri's ability to perform tasks with voice commands allows users to effortlessly multitask and access information without ever needing to touch their device.

2. Siri and Apple HomeKit Integration

With the increasing popularity of smart homes, Siri's integration with Apple's HomeKit is a key element of its role within the Apple ecosystem. HomeKit is a framework that allows users to control smart home devices from various manufacturers using their Apple devices. Through Siri, users can easily control lighting, thermostats, locks, cameras, and more, with simple voice commands. For instance, users can state, "Hey Siri, turn off the lights in the living room," and Siri will communicate with compatible HomeKit-enabled devices to execute the command. The seamless integration of Siri and HomeKit empowers users to effortlessly manage their smart home devices without needing to navigate through multiple apps.

3. Siri for Accessibility

Siri is designed to be inclusive and accessible to all users, including those with disabilities. With its voice command capabilities, Siri allows individuals with limited mobility or vision impairments to interact with their Apple devices effectively. Users can leverage Siri to perform tasks such as composing messages, making calls, controlling smart home devices, accessing information, and more. Siri's accessibility features break down the barrier between users and their devices, enabling a more inclusive and personalized digital experience.

4. Siri and Third-Party App Integration

Siri's usefulness extends beyond Apple's native apps. With the introduction of SiriKit, developers can integrate their third-party apps with Siri, allowing users to perform specific actions within those apps using voice commands. This integration enables users to control various aspects of their digital life, including ordering a ride through a ridesharing app, sending money via payment apps, playing music from a preferred streaming service, and more. As Siri continues to expand its compatibility with third-party apps, it enhances the overall versatility and utility of the virtual assistant, making it an indispensable tool within the Apple ecosystem.

5. Siri on Different Apple Devices

Siri's ubiquity across various Apple devices amplifies its impact within the ecosystem. Whether it's an iPhone, iPad, Mac, Apple Watch, or even an Apple TV, Siri is there to assist users across all these devices. Users can access Siri effortlessly by activating the "Hey Siri" command or by long-pressing the dedicated Siri button available on many Apple devices. The synchronization and continuity of Siri on different devices ensure a seamless user experience that seamlessly transitions between devices, allowing users to employ Siri based on their preferences and needs.

In conclusion, Siri plays an indispensable role within the Apple ecosystem, serving as an intelligent personal assistant, a gateway to home automation, an accessibility tool, and an integration hub for third-party apps. From managing tasks to controlling smart home devices and accessing information across a range of Apple devices, Siri's capabilities empower users to command their digital world with ease. As Siri continues to evolve and integrate with new technologies, its role within the Apple ecosystem steadily strengthens, offering users an ever-improving and personalized experience.

# Chapter 2: Getting Started with Siri

Amidst these chapter, we will dive into the exciting world of Siri and explore how to get started with this intelligent virtual assistant. Whether you are a fresh Apple device user or simply looking to make the most out of Siri's capabilities, this comprehensive guide will provide you with easy-to-follow instructions and tips. So, let's get started and uncover the true potential of Siri.

Understanding Siri:

Siri, short for Speech Interpretation and Recognition Interface, is Apple's cutting-edge virtual assistant available on iPhones, iPads, Macs, Apple Watches, and more. Siri helps you perform numerous tasks hands-free, simply by using your voice. Whether you want to send a message, make a call, set reminders, play music, answer questions, or get directions, Siri is here to assist you every step of the way.

Activating Siri:

To activate Siri, simply follow these steps based on the Apple device you own:

For iPhones and iPads:

1. Navigate to "Settings" on your home screen.

2. Scroll down and tap on "Siri & Search. "

3. Toggle the "Listen for 'Hey Siri'" switch to enable Siri to activate when you say the key phrase, "Hey Siri. " (*Note: This feature may not be available on older Apple devices. )

4. Additionally, you can also choose to enable "Allow Siri When Locked" to use Siri even when your device is locked.

For Macs:

1. Click on the Apple menu in the top-left corner of your screen and select "System Preferences. "

2. Click on "Keyboard" and then select the "Siri" tab.

3. Check the box next to "Enable Ask Siri" to activate Siri on your Mac.

For Apple Watches:

1. Wake your Apple Watch by tapping on the display or raising your wrist.

2. To activate Siri, simply say "Hey Siri" or press and hold the Digital Crown.

Interacting with Siri:

Once Siri is activated, you can start interacting with it by giving voice commands. To achieve the best results while using Siri, keep the following tips in mind:

1. Begin your Siri command with the phrase "Hey Siri" on your iPhone, iPad, or Apple Watch. On Macs, use the keyboard shortcut "Command + Spacebar" or click on the Siri icon in the menu bar.

2. Speak clearly and naturally, ensuring there is a proper distance from the device's microphone for optimal voice recognition.

3. Make your commands or questions concise and specific. Siri works better when given straightforward instructions.

Exploring Siri's Capabilities:

Siri boasts a wide range of capabilities designed to simplify your daily life. Below are some exciting ways to leverage Siri's functionality:

1. Setting Alarms, Timers, and Reminders:

- Set alarms by saying, "Hey Siri, set an alarm for 7 AM. "

- Create timers using commands like "Hey Siri, set a timer for 10 minutes. "

- Set reminders with voice prompts such as "Hey Siri, remind me to buy groceries tomorrow at 5 PM. "

2. Making Calls and Sending Messages:

- Dial a contact by saying, "Hey Siri, call [contact name]. "

- Send messages by stating, "Hey Siri, send a message to [contact name]. "

3. Managing Calendar Events:

- Schedule appointments by asking Siri, "Hey Siri, create a reminder for my dentist appointment on Friday at 2 PM. "

- Get information about existing events with commands like "Hey Siri, what's on my calendar today. "

4. Getting Directions:

- Find your way around by saying, "Hey Siri, give me directions to [location] using Apple Maps. "

5. Enjoying Music:

- Easily access your favorite music by requesting commands like "Hey Siri, play my favorite playlist. "

6. Checking Weather and News:

- Stay updated by inquiring, "Hey Siri, what's the weather like today. "

- Get the latest news by asking Siri, "Hey Siri, what are the latest headlines. "

Customizing Siri:

Siri can be tailored to suit your preferences. For customization options, follow these steps based on your device:

For iPhones and iPads:

1. Open "Settings" on your home screen.

2. Scroll down and tap on "Siri & Search. "

3. Here, you can enable various preferences like "Listen for 'Hey Siri,'" "Press Side Button for Siri," and "Allow Siri When Locked. "

For Macs:

1. Click on the Apple menu in the top-left corner of your screen and select "System Preferences. "

2. Click on "Siri" to access customization options. You've now laid the foundation for effectively using Siri. Amidst these chapter, we explored how to activate Siri on various Apple devices, provided tips for interacting with the assistant, and discovered the multitude of tasks Siri can help you accomplish effortlessly. In the next chapter, we will delve deeper into Siri's advanced features, including integration with third-party apps and enhancing your productivity. So, get ready to unlock more possibilities with Siri as we journey together in this exploration of Apple's revolutionary virtual assistant.

# 2.1 Enabling and Setting Up Siri

Siri, the virtual assistant developed by Apple, provides a convenient and interactive way to interact with your Apple devices. Whether you want to set reminders, send text messages, ask for directions, play music, or control your smart home devices, Siri can assist you efficiently. Amidst this chapter, we will explore the steps to enable and set up Siri on your Apple device, empowering you to make the most out of this remarkable virtual assistant.

1. Compatibility:

Before diving into the setup process, it is crucial to ensure that your Apple device supports Siri. Siri is available on iPhones, iPads, Apple Watches, Apple TVs, and Mac computers. However, keep in mind that some older device models may not support Siri's advanced features. Checking Apple's official website will provide you with a comprehensive list of supported devices.

2. Enabling Siri:

To enable Siri, you must start by accessing your device's settings. On an iPhone or iPad, navigate to "Settings," while on a Mac computer, open "System Preferences. " On an Apple Watch, tap the "Settings" app, and on an Apple TV, go to "Settings. "

3. On an iPhone or iPad:

a. Find and tap the "Siri & Search" option.

b. Toggle the button next to "Listen for 'Hey Siri'" to enable this convenient voice activation feature.

c. You can also toggle the "Press Side Button for Siri" option, allowing you to summon Siri by pressing and holding the side button on your device.

4. On a Mac computer:

a. Select the "Siri" icon within the System Preferences window.

b. Tick the checkbox labeled "Enable Siri. "

c. Optionally, choose the desired voice-interrupt settings from the "Voice Feedback" dropdown menu.

5. On an Apple Watch:

a. Open the "Settings" app on your Apple Watch.

b. Find and tap on "Siri. "

c. Toggle the switch adjacent to "Hey Siri" to turn on this feature.

d. You can also enable the "Raise to Speak" option, which makes Siri active by merely raising your wrist and speaking.

6. On an Apple TV:

a. Go to "Settings" using the Apple TV remote.

b. Choose "Siri & Search. "

c. Toggle the button next to "Press Siri Remote for Siri" to enable Siri on your Apple TV.

7. Fine-tuning Siri's Language and Accent:

Apple allows users to personalize Siri by selecting their preferred language and accent. Siri supports multiple languages, and within those languages, you can choose from various accents. These settings can be customized in the "Siri & Search" section (on iPhones, iPads, and Apple Watches) or the Siri preferences window (on Mac computers).

8. Training Siri to Recognize your Voice (iPhone, iPad, and Mac only):

Siri's voice recognition capabilities can be enhanced by training it to recognize your voice. This increases accuracy, privacy, and reduces the chances of accidental activations by others. In the Siri settings, you will find an option called "Set Up 'Hey Siri'", which will guide you through the voice training process step-by-step.

9. Finalizing Siri Activation Preferences:

After enabling Siri, it is essential to choose the preferred method to activate it. Whether you want Siri to respond to voice commands only or opt for a combination of voice activation and button press, this customization ensures a seamless integration with your individual preferences. Feel free to experiment with different settings and options until you find the combination that works best for you. Now that your Siri is ready for interaction, we can move on to the next chapter, where we will explore some of the fundamental commands and tasks you can perform with Siri. By mastering these capabilities, you will unlock Siri's full potential as your reliable virtual assistant.

# 2.2 Activating Siri: Voice Commands and Methods

Amidst the information in this chapter, we will explore the various ways to activate Apple Siri using voice commands and methods. Siri, the intelligent personal assistant on Apple devices, is designed to provide users with a seamless and hands-free experience. By understanding and mastering the activation methods for Siri, you can make the most of this powerful tool. So, let's dive in and explore the different ways to activate Siri effortlessly.

1. The Home Button Method:

The most common way to activate Siri is by using the home button on your Apple device. Follow these simple steps to activate Siri using the home button method:

Step 1: Ensure your Apple device is awake and unlocked.

Step 2: Press and hold the home button for a few seconds.

Step 3: Once you see the Siri interface appear, speak your voice command.

2. The Side Button Method (For Devices Without a Home Button):

If you own an iPhone X or newer models without a physical home button, utilize the side button method to activate Siri. Here's how you can do it:

Step 1: Ensure your iPhone is awake and unlocked.

Step 2: Press and hold the side button (also known as the power button) on the device.

Step 3: When the Siri interface appears, speak your command.

3. The "Hey Siri" Functionality:

Apple has integrated a hands-free feature into Siri known as "Hey Siri." By enabling this functionality, you can seamlessly activate Siri using just your voice. To set up and use "Hey Siri":

Step 1: Open the Settings app on your Apple device.

Step 2: Scroll down and tap on Siri & Search.

Step 3: Enable the "Listen for 'Hey Siri'" toggle switch.

Note: In older devices, this feature may require being connected to a power source. On devices like the iPhone 6 and earlier, keep your device plugged in or charging for "Hey Siri" to function.

4. AirPods and Headphone Activation:

If you often use Apple's AirPods or any supported headphones with Siri, you'll be glad to know there are specific voice commands to activate Siri conveniently. Here's how:

Step 1: Ensure your AirPods or compatible headphones are connected to your Apple device.

Step 2: Double-tap on either AirPod or press and hold the call/play button on your compatible headphones.

Step 3: Siri will be activated, and you can speak your command right away.

It's worth noting that these activation methods may vary slightly across different Apple devices, iOS versions, or settings configurations. To explore specific details tailored to your device, refer to the official Apple documentation or your device's user manual.

In conclusion, activating Siri using voice commands and methods is fundamental to accessing the extensive capabilities of the Siri assistant. Whether you prefer using the home button method, the side button method, or prefer hands-free interaction with "Hey Siri," mastering these techniques will ensure a smooth and efficient Siri experience. Additionally, utilizing Siri with AirPods or supported headphones can bring about more convenience in scenarios where you are on the go or need to keep your device in your pocket or bag.

Now that you understand the various activation methods for Siri, let's move on to exploring how Siri can help you with tasks, provide useful information, and enhance your daily life in the subsequent chapters.

# 2.3 Customizing Siri Settings and Preferences

Customizing Siri Settings and Preferences
 In the previous section, we discussed the basics of using Siri and getting comfortable with its features. Now, let's dive deeper into the realm of customization and explore the plethora of settings and preferences that Apple Siri offers, allowing you to personalize your Siri experience to your exact liking.

2.3.1 Language and Region Preferences

One of the first settings you might want to tweak is Siri's language preference. By default, Siri is set to use the language associated with your device's region settings. However, you can change this to any supported language of your choice. To do so, follow these steps:

1. Open the "Settings" app on your Apple device.
2. Scroll down and tap on "Siri & Search."
3. Select "Language" and choose the desired language from the list.

Changing the language will impact Siri's ability to understand and respond to your commands in that particular language. Additionally, selecting a new language may require a download of necessary language data, so ensure that you have a stable internet connection.

Similarly, you can adjust your region preferences under the same "Siri & Search" settings menu, allowing Siri to provide localized content, recommendations, and information based on your chosen region.

2.3.2 Siri Voice Preferences

Another area where you can customize Siri significantly is its voice. Siri offers a range of different voices, each with its unique characteristics and styles. Here's how you can change Siri's voice:

1. Open the "Settings" app on your Apple device.
2. Scroll down and tap on "Siri & Search."
3. Select "Siri Voice."

Once there, you'll be presented with a list of available voices, categorized by supported languages. Tap on any voice you find appealing, and Siri will switch to that new voice right away. Experimenting with different voices can bring a refreshing change to your interaction with Siri.

Additionally, Siri also offers options for voice feedback, including "Always On," "Control with Ring Switch," and "Hands-Free Only". These settings determine how and when Siri speaks to you. Whether you want to enable Siri's voice feedback explicitly or limit it to certain conditions, these options allow for highly-personalized preferences.

2.3.3 Hey Siri Settings

The phrase "Hey Siri" is Apple's famous activation phrase for Siri. You can invoke Siri simply by saying "Hey Siri" without needing to press any buttons. However, before utilizing this hands-free feature, you need to enable it and specify under what conditions Siri should respond.

To customize Hey Siri, follow these steps:

1. Open the "Settings" app on your Apple device.
2. Scroll down and tap on "Siri & Search."
3. Select "Hey Siri."

On the "Hey Siri" settings page, you can choose when your device will respond to the Hey Siri command. You have two main options here: enabling Hey Siri when your device is either connected to a power source (charging) or always, regardless of charging. Ensure you select the option that seamlessly harmonizes with your regular usage patterns and preferences.

Moreover, Hey Siri allows voice recognition training to enhance its accuracy. Tap on "Hey Siri" and follow the steps to train Siri to recognize your voice accurately.

2.3.4 App Support and Suggestions

Siri's integration with various apps greatly enhances its capabilities and usefulness. You can customize the apps that Siri can access and perform tasks with. Here's how to manage Siri's app support preferences:

1. Open the "Settings" app on your Apple device.
2. Scroll down and tap on "Siri & Search."
3. Select "App Support."

Within these settings menu, you can choose from a range of apps installed on your device. Ensure the toggle switches next to the apps are turned on for desired app integration with Siri.

Furthermore, this menu also presents an option to allow or disallow the "Siri Suggestions" feature. When enabled, Siri Observes and learns your app usage behavior, then provides intelligent recommendations, shortcuts, and relevant actions based on your patterns.

2.3.5 Contact and Personal Information

Ideally, Siri should have access to your complete contact and personal information to assist you efficiently. To check if Siri has access to your desired data or grant it access, follow these steps:

1. Open the "Settings" app on your Apple device.

2. Scroll down and tap on "Siri & Search."

3. Select "My Information."

Under "My Information," you'll be presented with a list of contacts saved on your device. Choose your name or the contact containing your personal information. This grants Siri access to your details, ensuring it can fulfill requests like "Call my dad," "Send a text to my sister," or any other command that requires knowledge of your contacts.

Remember, Siri respects your privacy and will not access or use any data without your consent.

2.3.6 Siri Suggestions on Lock Screen

Siri Suggestions on the lock screen can be quite handy, providing instant access to relevant apps or shortcuts without the need to unlock your device. You can control whether Siri Suggestions should be displayed when your device is locked. To manage this setting, follow these steps:

1. Open the "Settings" app on your Apple device.

2. Scroll down and tap on "Siri & Search."

3. Select "Suggestions on Lock Screen."

Under this setting, you have three options to choose from:

- Enabled: Siri Suggestions are displayed when the device is locked, offering efficient accessibility.

- Disabled: Siri Suggestions are entirely hidden when the device is locked.

- While Unlocked: Siri Suggestions are visible once you have unlocked your device.

Make a selection here based on your privacy requirements and convenience.

3. Conclusion

Customizing Siri settings and preferences helps tailor Apple's intelligent virtual assistant to fit your individual needs seamlessly. Whether it's changing the language, altering the voice, configuring Hey Siri responsiveness, app integration, or managing personal data access, don't hesitate to explore the options until you achieve the perfect setting to enhance your Siri experience. So, dive into the Siri settings menu and customize Siri as per your liking, empowering you with an assistant that's perfectly aligned with your needs and preferences.

# Chapter 3: Mastering Basic Functions

E ntailed within this chapter, we will delve deeper into the basic functions of Apple Siri and help you take full advantage of its capabilities. Siri is here to assist you with various tasks and provide valuable information, making your life simpler and more convenient. By mastering these fundamental features, you can unlock Siri's potential to simplify your daily routine and enhance your overall user experience.

1. Setting Up Siri:

To begin, let's ensure Siri is set up correctly on your Apple device. Open the Settings app and navigate to Siri & Search. Ensure that the toggle switch for "Listen for 'Hey Siri'" is enabled. You may also desire to enable Siri with the side or the Home button.

2. Initiating Siri:

The creation of virtual assistants, like Siri, exponentially improved the way we interact with our devices. Activating Siri is convenient and hassle-free. You can initiate Siri through voice commands using the phrases "Hey Siri," which works with most devices, or "Hey Siri, how can I help you. "

3. Asking Questions and Getting Information:

One of Siri's primary functions is providing you with information. You can ask Siri questions on a wide array of topics ranging from general knowledge to specific facts. For instance, you could say, "Hey Siri, what's the weather like today. " or "Hey Siri, who won the last Academy Awards. ". Siri will respond promptly, offering accurate and up-to-date information read aloud or displayed on your device's screen.

4. Setting Reminders and Alarms:

Managing your time effectively is crucial, and Siri can be an invaluable ally in accomplishing this. You can ask Siri to set reminders or alarms for important tasks or events. For example, try saying, "Hey Siri, set a reminder to call the dentist tomorrow at 10 AM. " Siri will create the reminder for you, sending you timely notifications to ensure you never miss an important event.

5. Sending Messages and Making Calls:

Another essential function Siri provides is the ability to send messages and make phone calls. This feature is particularly helpful when you're occupied or can't directly access your device. You can ask Siri to send a message to a specific contact or call someone by saying, "Hey Siri, send a message to John saying I'll be there soon," or "Hey Siri, call Mom. " Siri will perform the task on your behalf, generating the message or initiating the call effortlessly.

6. Managing Calendar and Events:

Siri helps you organize and keep track of your appointments, ensuring you remain on top of your schedule. Ask Siri to schedule a meeting, add an event to your calendar, or make adjustments to existing appointments. You can say, "Hey Siri, schedule a meeting with the team on Friday at 3 PM," or "Hey Siri, move my dentist appointment to next Tuesday at 11 AM. " Siri will make the necessary updates, ensuring your calendar is accurate and up to date.

7. Control System Settings:

Siri also provides a convenient way to control certain system settings on your Apple device. You can ask Siri to enable or disable Wi-Fi, Bluetooth, airplane mode, or adjust screen brightness. Simply say, "Hey Siri, turn on Wi-Fi," or "Hey Siri, decrease screen brightness. " Siri will promptly adjust these settings according to your preferences, saving you time and effort.

Conclusion:

Entailed within this chapter, we explored the basic functions of Apple Siri and its potential to simplify various daily tasks. From retrieving information and setting reminders to sending messages and managing calendar events, Siri proves to be an invaluable virtual assistant. Remember, mastering these fundamental features opens the door to a more efficient and convenient user experience. As you become familiar with Siri's capabilities, you will discover new ways to integrate it into your routine, heightening your productivity and making everyday life more enjoyable.

# 3.1 Making Calls and Sending Messages with Siri

One of the most useful features of Apple's Siri is its ability to help you make calls and send messages using just your voice. Gone are the days of fumbling around to find contacts or struggling with the tiny keyboard on your phone. Siri simplifies these tasks for you, making them effortless and hands-free. Amidst this section, we will explore how to utilize Siri's capabilities to easily make calls and send messages.

To start, ensure that Siri is enabled on your device. You can do this by going to "Settings," selecting "Siri & Search," and toggling on the "Listen for 'Hey Siri'" option. You can also enable Siri by pressing and holding the Side button or Home button on your device, depending on the model.

To make a call with Siri, begin by saying "Hey Siri" or pressing the activation button. Once Siri is active, simply say "Call [Contact's Name]" or "Dial [Phone Number]." Siri will then initiate the call for you. For example, saying "Hey Siri, call John" will prompt Siri to dial John's number and establish a connection for you. If you have multiple contacts with the same name, Siri may ask you to confirm the specific person you want to call.

Sending messages with Siri is equally effortless. Just start with "Hey Siri" or by pressing the activation button. Then, say "Send a message to [Contact's Name]" or "Text [Contact's Name]." Siri will inquire about the message content and dictate it once you've approved or edited it. For example, saying "Hey Siri, send a message to Lisa" will prompt Siri to ask for the message content, and you could respond, "Tell her I'll be running a few minutes late."

Additionally, Siri allows you to send messages using popular messaging apps like WhatsApp, Telegram, or Messenger. You can specify the app you prefer to use in your command. For instance, you can say, "Send a WhatsApp message to Steve" or "Text Sarah on Messenger." Siri will ensure your message reaches the intended recipient through the chosen app.

Siri's flexibility extends further by allowing you to make hands-free calls and interact with messages while driving. When connected to your car's Bluetooth or CarPlay, Siri enables you to place calls without ever touching your iPhone. By simply stating "Hey Siri" or pressing the activation button, you can instruct Siri to call someone from your contacts list or dial a specific number. This feature ensures your safety while driving by keeping your hands on the steering wheel and your focus on the road.

Furthermore, Siri can read out your incoming messages aloud, providing a convenient and safe way to stay updated without detracting your attention from driving. You can set Siri to announce messages whenever they arrive or activate Siri manually and ask to read new messages. Siri will proceed to read the message content, including details such as the sender's name and the message itself. If you wish to reply, Siri will patiently await your dictations and send your response when instructed.

Siri also helps with other incoming alerts, such as missed calls or voicemails. If you're unable to check these notifications immediately, you can ask Siri to review them for you at a later time. By saying "Hey Siri, do I have any missed calls?" or "Hey Siri, check my voicemail," Siri will promptly provide you with details about any latest events you might have missed.

It's worth noting that Siri relies on accurate contact details within your device for smooth call placement and messaging. Make sure your contacts are up-to-date, including phone numbers and email addresses. Siri can also utilize the relationships feature to recognize your friends and family. Assigning relationships to your contacts (e.g., "mom," "dad," "brother") will allow Siri to better understand your instructions, such as "Call my brother" or "Text mom." You can teach Siri these relationships by editing the contact information or explicitly instructing Siri to assign a relationship when prompted.

Using Siri's capabilities to make calls and send messages not only streamlines your communication process but also safeguards your productivity and overall well-being. By harnessing its hands-free utilities and compatibility with various messaging apps, Siri unlocks a new level of convenience and efficiency. With Siri as your personal assistant, you can rely on its reliability, versatility, and intuitive features to make calls and exchange messages with ease. Embrace the power of voice commands with Apple Siri and experience the true potential of effortless communication.

# 3.2 Setting Alarms, Timers, and Reminders

Setting Alarms, Timers, and Reminders with Apple Siri

Amid this section, we will explore the features and capabilities of Apple Siri in regards to setting alarms, timers, and reminders. Siri offers a convenient way to manage your time, ensuring you don't miss important events, deadlines, or appointments. Whether you need a gentle reminder to wake up in the morning or a timer to monitor the cooking process, Siri has got you covered. Let's dive into the world of setting alarms, timers, and reminders with Siri.

1. Alarms:

Alarms are a reliable way to wake up in the morning or get timely notifications for any specific event. Siri can help you set alarms with ease and flexibility. Simply follow these steps:

1. Invoke Siri by pressing and holding the home button or using the "Hey Siri" command if configured.

2. Once Siri is active, say "Set an alarm for [time]. " For example, you can say, "Set an alarm for 7 AM" or "Set an alarm for 30 minutes from now. "

3. Siri will confirm the alarm setup and display the details for your review. If everything is correct, a tap on the confirm button will set the alarm.

Furthermore, Siri also allows you to manage your alarms. You can ask Siri to show your existing alarms, cancel a specific alarm, or modify the timing for an already set alarm. It's as simple as saying, "Show my alarms," "Cancel the 7 AM alarm," or "Change the 30 minutes from now alarm to 45 minutes from now. "

2. Timers:

Timers are excellent for effortless tracking of short-duration tasks, such as cooking or exercise routines. Siri can help you set timers without having to physically interact with your device. Here's how:

1. Activate Siri by holding the home button or using the "Hey Siri" command.

2. Give the voice command, "Set a timer for [duration]. " For instance, say, "Set a timer for 20 minutes" or "Set a timer for 1 hour and 30 minutes. "

3. Siri will acknowledge the timer and display it on your screen. You can also check the timer's status by asking Siri.

In addition to setting timers, Siri lets you cancel or modify existing timers. Just say, "Cancel the 20-minute timer," or "Change the 1-hour and 30-minute timer to 2 hours. "

3. Reminders:

Reminders are a versatile feature Siri offers to help you manage your tasks, errands, and appointments. Siri makes it effortless to create, modify, and view reminders based on your voice commands. Follow these steps to leverage Siri for reminders:

1. Activate Siri using the preferred method.

2. Say a phrase like, "Remind me to [task] at [time/day]. "

- You can even allocate locations for the reminder with commands like "Remind me to [task] when I leave home. "

3. Siri will confirm the reminder and display it for your review. You can modify or confirm the reminder as needed.

Siri also permits managing reminders through voice commands. For example, you can say, "Show me my reminders," "Mark [task] as complete," or "Move [task] to tomorrow. "

Conclusion:

In conclusion, Apple Siri serves as a fantastic personal assistant when it comes to setting alarms, timers, and reminders. The voice-activated commands provide convenience and flexibility in managing your time and tasks effectively. By following the steps mentioned above, you can harness the power of Siri and make sure you never miss important events or forget critical tasks. So, go ahead and explore Siri's alarm, timer, and reminder capabilities to experience a seamless time management solution.

# 3.3 Managing Calendar Events and Appointments

M anaging Calendar Events and Appointments
One of the most useful features of Apple Siri is its ability to help you effortlessly manage your calendar events and appointments. Gone are the days of having to manually type in every detail or constantly switch apps to add events. Siri saves you time and effort by allowing you to create and manage your calendar events through voice commands. Amidst the contents of this chapter, we will delve into the various ways you can leverage Siri to efficiently handle your busy schedule.

1. Creating New Events:

Siri allows you to easily add new events to your calendar without any hassle. For instance, you can simply say, "Hey Siri, create a meeting with John tomorrow from 2 PM to 3 PM." Siri will understand the command and create the event for you, automatically filling in the necessary details such as title, date, and time. If specific details are omitted, Siri will prompt you to provide the missing information.

2. Editing Events:

Sometimes, plans change or you may need to make modifications to your existing events. With Siri, you can effortlessly edit and update events on the go. For example, say, "Hey Siri, reschedule Monday's 5 PM meeting to Thursday at 2 PM." Siri will promptly understand your request, modify the event accordingly, and notify participants if required.

3. Checking Your Schedule:

To ensure you have a clear view of your upcoming events, you can rely on Siri as your personal assistant. Ask Siri questions like, "Hey Siri, what's on my schedule today?" or "Hey Siri, what appointments do I have tomorrow?" Siri will quickly retrieve the information and provide you with a detailed summary of your calendar.

4. Adding Invitations:

If you have an event that requires you to invite others, Siri can perform that task effortlessly. You can mentally offload the invitation process to Siri by saying something like, "Hey Siri, create a dinner invitation for Saturday at 7 PM and invite Jane, Peter, and Sarah." Siri will promptly generate the invitation, populate the relevant details, and send the invites on your behalf.

5. Managing Reminders:

Siri understands that reminders are an integral part of your schedule and can help you stay on top of important tasks. You can create reminders disguised as events by instructing Siri, "Hey Siri, add 'Buy groceries' to my calendar for tomorrow at 5 PM." Siri will cleverly convert your statement into an event and remind you of the task when the time arrives.

6. Getting Directions:

Siri combines its ability to manage appointments with its navigation features to provide you with a seamless experience. For example, if Siri has an event on your schedule with an associated location, you can ask Siri to "Give me directions to my next meeting." Siri will bring up the Maps app and guide you to your destination, optimally factoring in traffic and preferred routes.

7. Working with Third-Party Calendar Apps:

While Siri seamlessly connects with Apple's default Calendar app, it also plays nicely with third-party calendar apps. Whether you prefer Google Calendar, Outlook, or any other supported app, you can link your accounts and manage your events effortlessly through Siri. Simply ensure you've granted permissions and configured the necessary settings for Siri to access and modify events in these applications.

8. Confirmations and Notifications:

Lastly, Siri ensures you are regularly updated and notified about your upcoming events. For instance, if you enable notifications for your events, Siri will kindly remind you about them as the scheduled time approaches. Additionally, Siri can send you confirmations and reminders for events you have added, ensuring you never miss an important meeting or appointment.

Utilizing Siri to manage your calendar is a game-changer for staying organized and productive. Whether you need to create, edit, or check your schedule, Siri provides a hands-free and convenient solution to handle your events and appointments. By mastering these Siri capabilities, you can spend more time focusing on important tasks and leave the scheduling logistics to your digital assistant.

# Chapter 4: Productivity with Siri

A mid this chapter, we will explore how Apple Siri can be a powerful tool to enhance productivity in your daily life. Siri is not just a virtual assistant; it can also act as a personal assistant, helping you stay organized and efficient. By leveraging Siri's capabilities for task management, scheduling, reminders, and note-taking, you can save time and streamline your workflow. Amid this chapter, we will delve into the various productivity features of Siri and learn how to utilize them effectively.

Section 1: Managing Tasks:

One of the key productivity features of Siri is its ability to assist you in managing tasks. With Siri, you can create, modify, and organize your to-do lists effortlessly. Simply summon Siri and say commands like "Remind me to buy groceries" or "Create a task to call the client tomorrow at 10 am. " Siri will create reminders based on your input and automatically sync them with the Reminders app on your iPhone, iPad, or Mac.

You can also use Siri to view your upcoming tasks and check them off as you complete them. For instance, you can say, "What are my tasks for today. " or "Mark the grocery shopping task as completed. " Siri will help ensure that nothing important slips through the cracks.

Section 2: Scheduling and Calendar Management:

Siri's integration with the Calendar app makes it effortless to schedule appointments, set up meetings, and manage your calendar effectively. You can simply say commands like "Schedule a meeting with John at 2 pm on Tuesday" or "schedule a dental appointment for next Friday at 10 am. " Siri will interpret your request and create the corresponding events in your calendar.

Siri can also assist you in checking your upcoming events and provide details such as location, time, and any other information associated with the events. For example, by asking Siri, "What's on my schedule today. " or "When is my next meeting. ", you can quickly stay on top of your appointments and commitments.

Section 3: Taking Notes and Recall:

Taking quick notes or jotting down important information can sometimes be challenging in a busy workflow. But Siri can ease this process and help you maintain an organized note-taking system. Whether it's capturing an idea, making a grocery shopping list, or drafting a reminder, all you need to do is call upon Siri.

You can instruct Siri commands like "Create a note with the shopping list" or "Take a note reminding me to call Tom later. " Siri will instantly understand your request and create the notes in the Apple Notes app. These notes will be available on all your Apple devices, ensuring they are accessible whenever and wherever required. To retrieve a note, ask Siri to search for specific content within your notes and she will present the relevant results.

Section 4: Home Automation:

Beyond managing tasks, calendar, and notes, Siri can extend its productivity to controlling smart home devices that are compatible with Apple's HomeKit ecosystem. By integrating Siri with compatible smart devices, you can create routines and command Siri to perform tasks like turning off lights, adjusting thermostat settings, or even opening the garage door, all with a simple verbal prompt.

Conclusion:

With Siri's multitude of productivity features, managing tasks, scheduling appointments, taking notes, and controlling your smart home becomes a breeze. Apple Siri acts as an assistant that diligently listens to your commands and seamlessly integrates with your Apple devices to keep you organized and efficient. By harnessing the power of Siri's productivity features, you can optimize your daily workflow and focus on achieving your goals effectively.

# 4.1 Email Management and Dictation with Siri

In today's fast-paced world, managing our email efficiently is crucial for staying organized and on top of our business and personal communications. Apple Siri, the intelligent personal assistant, goes beyond simple voice commands and can help you effectively manage your email with ease. Housed within this chapter, we will delve into the realm of email management and dictate with Siri, uncovering its various features and capabilities, allowing you to handle your messages effortlessly.

One of the most prominent features Siri offers for email management is the ability to compose, reply, and read emails entirely hands-free. Whether you're busy preparing a meal in the kitchen or driving home from work, Siri allows you to stay connected without compromising your safety or convenience. To start composing an email, you can simply say, "Hey Siri, compose an email to [contact's name]." Siri will ask to confirm the recipient, after which you can dictate the subject and body of your email. Siri also offers advanced options like setting the priority level, adding attachments, or even requesting read receipts in supported email providers.

When reading emails with Siri, you can easily index through the messages in your inbox by uttering commands like "read my recent emails," "read the next email," or "read the previous email." Siri will promptly read out the sender, subject, and the body of the message, ensuring you stay updated, even when your hands are occupied. Furthermore, Siri can manage email threads by allowing you to reply to or forward a specific message within a conversation effortlessly. You can say "reply to this email," and Siri will guide you through the process while listing the message content, ensuring you address the correct part of the ongoing conversation.

As you become more acquainted with Siri's email management capabilities, you'll come to appreciate its intelligent filtering and organizing techniques. Siri can help you search your inbox, creating convenience and saving valuable time.

For example, uttering something like "Find emails from Jane about the project" will prompt Siri to display a list of relevant messages according to your request. You can filter your search based on specific criteria, such as senders, subjects, or timeframes, using natural language commands. Siri will promptly present the results in a user-friendly format, allowing you to quickly navigate through the search outcomes.

Beyond basic email management, Siri also provides dictation capabilities, allowing you to send emails without touching the keyboard. Dictating emails with Siri not only saves time, but it also ensures accurate transcription of your message. To dictate an email, begin by saying, "Hey Siri, dictate an email to [contact's name]." Siri will confirm the recipient, and then you can speak your message. While dictating, it's crucial to articulate clearly and enunciate punctuations like "comma" or "exclamation mark" to ensure smooth interpretation by Siri. After finishing your dictation, Siri will ask you to review the composed message before sending it, ensuring accuracy and avoiding any potential mistakes.

Furthermore, Siri supports textual editing commands, making it incredibly convenient for you to make modifications or corrections to the composed draft. Commence such edits by simply saying commands like "cap," "comma," "new paragraph," or "replace [word] with [new word]." This intelligent feature allows users to refine the content of their emails even after dictating them. You can achieve a polished final version without needing a physical keyboard, all thanks to Siri's novel capabilities.

It is worth mentioning that Siri's email management and dictation features may require certain configurations on your Apple device and may depend on your chosen email provider's compatibility. Therefore, it is valuable to familiarize yourself with the set-up and ensure the necessary authorizations are granted to Siri to access your email account and associated contacts. You may also need to verify that your chosen email client supports Siri integration. By taking these initial steps, you'll ensure a seamless experience harnessing the full potential of Siri's email management and dictation capabilities.

In conclusion, Siri brings a wealth of convenience and efficiency to the realm of email management and dictation. Its hands-free composition, intelligent inbox filtering, and voice-controlled search functionalities elevate the user experience, allowing you to manage your email effortlessly. The dictation feature eliminates the need to type emails, replacing it with a more natural and convenient method of communication. With Siri, staying organized, conducting efficient email exchanges, and ensuring accurate transcription has never been easier. So embrace the power of Siri and let it revolutionize the way you handle your email communications.

# 4.2 Note-Taking and List Creation

Note-taking and list creation are two prominent features that elevate the Siri experience and enhance productivity for Apple users. Utilizing Siri's powerful voice recognition capabilities, you can effortlessly capture important information and seamlessly organize your thoughts without fumbling with a pen and paper. Contained within this section, we will delve into the intricacies of note-taking and list creation with Siri, providing you with comprehensive guidance on leveraging these functionalities efficiently.

4.2.1 Creating Simple Notes

Siri offers a convenient and efficient method to create simple notes on your Apple devices. Whether you want to jot down quick ideas, grocery lists, or important reminders, Siri has your back. To create a note using Siri, follow these simple steps:

1. Activate Siri by holding down the Home button or saying, "Hey Siri," on devices that support this feature without button interaction.

2. Once Siri is activated, you can ask it to create a note by saying phrases like "Create a note," or "Make a note."

3. Siri will prompt you to dictate the content of your note. Speak naturally and clearly, and Siri will accurately transcribe your voice into text.

4. After completing your note, Siri will ask you to provide a title for easy identification later. Mention a title in a clear and concise manner.

5. Siri will confirm your note's creation and add it to the default "Notes" app on your device.

It is worth noting that if you have multiple notes in the same session, Siri will amalgamate them into a single note unless specified otherwise. Therefore, ensure you specify different titles or mention "new note" between individual notes to preserve their independence.

4.2.2 Organizing Notes

The "Notes" app on your Apple device provides robust organizational features to help you manage your growing collection of notes efficiently. Siri seamlessly integrates with these functionalities, allowing you to effortlessly navigate and find specific notes in mere seconds. Here are some ways to organize your notes effectively using Siri:

1. Renaming Notes: If you want to provide more descriptive or intuitive titles to your notes, you can ask Siri to rename them. Activate Siri and say phrases such as "Rename note" or "Change note title" followed by the specific note's original and new titles. Siri will identify the note and promptly update its title.

2. Finding Notes: Siri can assist you in locating specific notes, even if you have an extensive library. Activate Siri and say phrases like "Find note about [topic]" or "Search for note with [keyword]." Siri will swiftly scan your notes and generate relevant results based on your inquiry.

3. Organizing into Folders: To keep your notes neatly organized, you can create and manage folders within the "Notes" app. Use Siri to create a new folder by saying phrases such as "Create a new folder" or "Make a folder." You can then move notes into folders using Siri, such as "Move note X to folder Y."

4. Syncing with iCloud: Siri ensures that your notes remain accessible across all your Apple devices through iCloud sync. So whether you're using Siri on your iPhone, iPad, or Mac, your notes will seamlessly sync, allowing you to access your important information from anywhere.

4.2.3 Creating Lists and To-Do Items

Apart from simple note-taking, Siri can also facilitate the creation of lists and to-do items, further streamlining your workflow and organization. With Siri's assistance, you can compile shopping lists, essential tasks, travel itineraries, and much more. Follow these steps:

1. Invoke Siri through the Home button or voice command on applicable devices.

2. To create a list or to-do item, say phrases such as "Create a shopping list" or "Make a to-do item."

3. Siri will ask you to dictate the initial item on the list, which you can narrate precisely and clearly.

4. After each item, indicate that you wish to add more by saying "Add more," or proceed to finalize the list by saying "Done" or "That's it."

Siri will promptly create the list and store it in your "Reminders" app, enabling you to refer to it whenever necessary. Similar to notes, you can efficiently organize your lists and sync them via iCloud for seamless accessibility on all your Apple devices.

### 4.2.4 Managing Lists and To-Do Items

Managing your lists and to-do items with Siri is just as simple and intuitive as creating them. Siri provides an array of capabilities to ensure you remain on top of your tasks with ease. Here's how to manage your lists effectively:

1. Adding to Existing Lists: If you have an existing list, Siri can help you add additional items seamlessly. Activate Siri and say phrases such as "Add [item] to [list name]" or simply "Add [item] to my list." Siri will identify the list mentioned and add the new item to it.

2. Checking Off or Deleting Items: When you have completed a task or wish to remove an item from your list, Siri offers efficient commands to check items off or delete them. Activate Siri and say "Check off [item]" or "Delete [item]," and Siri will promptly update your list accordingly.

3. Reminders and Alerts: Siri can set reminders based on specific lists or individual items. You can ask Siri to remind you about certain tasks or errands at specific times or locations. For example, you can say "Remind me to buy milk when I leave work" or "Remind me to call John at 5 pm." Siri will ensure you receive timely notifications and reminders.

Siri's note-taking capabilities and list creation options empower Apple users to capture thoughts, prioritize tasks, and streamline their daily activities effortlessly. By mastering these essential functionalities, you can enhance your productivity, stay organized, and make the most of Siri's ever-present virtual assistant expertise.

# 4.3 Using Siri for Navigation and Directions

Using Siri for Navigation and Directions

One of the incredible features of Apple Siri is its ability to assist users in navigation and provide helpful directions. With Siri, your iPhone becomes a personal navigator that can guide you through unfamiliar territories while keeping your hands free and your focus on the road. Whether you're navigating through a metropolis or planning a road trip, Siri can be your trusted co-pilot. Among these section, we will explore various aspects of using Siri for navigation and directions.

Starting Siri Navigation

To begin using Siri for navigation, you can simply activate Siri by holding down the home button on your iPhone or saying, "Hey Siri" if your device supports the hands-free feature. Once Siri is ready, you can ask it to assist you with directions to your desired location. For example, you could say, "Siri, how do I get to Central Park?"

Siri's Integration with Maps

Siri seamlessly integrates with Apple Maps. It recognizes the commands related to navigation and instantly launches the Maps app to provide you with turn-by-turn directions. This integration allows Siri to utilize the extensive mapping data and real-time traffic information available on your iPhone. Consequently, not only does Siri guide you with directions, but it can also suggest the best routes based on current traffic conditions.

Multiple Ways to Request Directions

Siri understands that users may have different preferences when requesting directions. You can ask Siri for directions using various commands and questions. For instance, you can try asking Siri, "What's the fastest way to reach Times Square?" or "Navigate me to the nearest police station." Siri understands the context and efficiently responds to your query.

Addressing Complex Route Queries

When searching for directions, Siri allows you to specify the type of transportation you prefer. For example, if you want to take public transportation, you can say, "Siri, show me the bus route to the airport." Siri will promptly display bus routes, including the corresponding schedules and transfers, making your journey planning even more convenient.

Navigating with Voice Assistance

Once your desired route and mode of transportation are confirmed, Siri will commence voice-guided navigation. It will seamlessly guide you with turn-by-turn instructions, ensuring you stay on the right path. Siri informs you in advance about upcoming maneuvers and provides details such as which lanes to be in or where to exit.

Interaction during Navigation

During your journey, Siri remains attentive to your voice commands. You can ask Siri questions such as, "How much longer until we arrive?" or "Siri, find a gas station nearby." Siri swiftly responds and respects the ongoing navigation by displaying additional information or making suggestions without interrupting or disturbing your path.

Voice Command Customization

Siri also offers voice command personalization. When using Siri frequently for navigation, take a moment to configure your preferences. Navigate to your device settings, locate Siri & Search, and open the App Shortcuts section. Here, you can create custom voice commands such as "Take me home" or "Let's drive." By personalizing these commands, you can make Siri easily recognize your voice while enhancing your navigation experience.

Exploring Points of Interest

In addition to providing navigation, Siri can help you explore points of interest along your route. For instance, while en route to a destination, you might ask Siri, "What are some highly rated restaurants in this area?" Siri will display a list of the best restaurants nearby, complete with reviews contributed by other users.

Unlocking Advanced Filters

What makes Siri for navigation truly dynamic is its advanced filtering options. You can tell Siri to search for specific types of businesses or add specific criteria to your search query. Consider uttering commands like "Find a Chinese restaurant offering delivery" or "Show me gas stations with the cheapest fuel prices." Siri diligently filters through vast information available and promptly offers you tailored results.

In summary, Siri serves as an indispensable tool when it comes to navigation and directions. It seamlessly combines voice recognition, powerful mapping technology, and real-time traffic data to offer a comprehensive and user-friendly navigation experience. Whether you require directions to a destination, assistance with public transportation, or exploration of nearby points of interest, Siri is always ready to guide you along the way. So, the next time you embark on a journey, trust Siri to be your virtual co-pilot, making the experience more enjoyable and stress-free.

# Chapter 5: Entertainment and Media

Amidst this chapter, we will explore the exciting world of entertainment and media with the help of Apple Siri. Siri is more than just a digital assistant; it can assist you in finding and enjoying various forms of entertainment, such as streaming movies and TV shows, playing music, and keeping up with the latest news. Whether you want to unwind after a long day or stay updated with the latest media trends, Siri will be your perfect companion. So, let's dive in and discover the plethora of entertainment options Siri has in store for you.

1. Discovering Streaming Content:

One of Siri's key features is its ability to help you find and enjoy your favorite movies and TV shows. Siri integrates with popular streaming services like Apple TV+, Netflix, Amazon Prime Video, and more. Simply initiate Siri by saying, "Hey Siri," followed by your request. For example, you can say, "Hey Siri, find romantic comedies on Apple TV+," and Siri will display relevant results for you to choose from. Siri can also assist in playing specific episodes of your favorite TV shows or movies.

2. Music Playback and Discovery:

Siri is your go-to assistant for playing music. You can request Siri to play a specific song, album, artist, or genre simply by asking, "Hey Siri, play [song/album/artist/genre]. " Siri will promptly fulfill your request by playing the requested content from your chosen music service, such as Apple Music or Spotify. Moreover, Siri can help you discover new songs based on your preferences. You can say, "Hey Siri, recommend some rock songs," and Siri will curate a personalized list for you.

3. Examining News and Podcasts:

Siri also acts as an outstanding source for keeping up with current events and the latest news. You can ask Siri about specific topics, such as sports, technology, finance, and more, by saying, "Hey Siri, give me the latest news on [topic]. " Siri will fetch news snippets from various sources, ensuring you remain informed. Furthermore, Siri makes it easy to access and play your favorite podcasts. Just ask Siri, "Hey Siri, play the latest episode of [podcast name]," and it will take care of the rest.

4. Book Recommendations and Reading Assistance:

Besides entertainment in the form of movies, music, and news, Siri can assist you in exploring the fascinating realm of literature. You can ask Siri for book recommendations by saying, "Hey Siri, suggest a thriller novel," and it will provide you with a list of recommendations based on your taste. Siri can also be your reading companion by opening books and helping you with certain reading actions. You can say, "Hey Siri, open iBooks and start reading [book title]," and Siri will commence your reading journey.

5. Gaming Assistance and Fun:

While Siri mainly focuses on media consumption, it can also offer some entertainment of its own. You can engage in interactive games and quizzes with Siri by saying, "Hey Siri, let's play a game. " Siri will provide you with various gaming options like trivia, puzzles, and word games. Additionally, you can explore Siri's sense of humor by asking it fun and light-hearted questions. Siri's amusing responses are sure to bring a smile to your face.

Conclusion:

With Siri as your potent ally, accessing entertainment and media has never been easier. From watching movies and TV shows to playing your favorite songs, staying updated with the news, exploring new book genres, and engaging in interactive games, Siri offers a range of opportunities to enhance your leisure time. Its seamless integration with various entertainment services and its ability to comprehend natural language make interacting with Siri effortless and enjoyable. So, get ready to embark on an adventure with Siri and unlock the vast world of entertainment and media.

# 5.1 Playing Music, Podcasts, and Audiobooks

Playing Music, Podcasts, and Audiobooks with Apple Siri
Listening to your favorite music, catching up on the latest podcasts, or delving into captivating audiobooks can be a delightful experience with Apple Siri. Siri, Apple's virtual assistant, allows you to effortlessly control your audio content with just your voice. Amidst the contents of this chapter, we will explore the various ways Siri can enhance your music, podcasts, and audiobook experience, providing you with a step-by-step guide to make the most out of Siri's capabilities.

1. Controlling Music:

Music enhances our lives, sets the mood, and transports us to different moments. Siri makes it incredibly convenient to access your music library and control playback without even lifting a finger. Here's how you can get started:

1. 1 Playing Songs:

Start by invoking Siri using your preferred activation method, such as saying "Hey Siri" or holding the home button. Then, you can use the following commands:

- "Play [song name] by [artist name]. "
- "Play music by [artist name]. "
- "Play the latest [genre] songs. "
- "Play my favorite songs. "

1. 2 Creating Playlists:

Siri can also help you organize and create playlists effortlessly. Simply ask Siri:

- "Create a new playlist named [playlist name]. "
- "Add this song to [playlist name]. "
- "Add [song name] to the [playlist name] playlist. "

1. 3 Controlling Playback:

Once your music is playing, Siri offers seamless control over playback options. Some handy commands include:

- "Pause the music. "
- "Resume the music. "
- "Skip this song. "
- "Play the previous song. "
- "Shuffle the playlist. "
- "Repeat this song/playlist. "

2. Exploring Podcasts:

Podcasts have become increasingly popular, providing an avenue to learn new things, dive into captivating stories, and stay updated with the latest news. Siri simplifies the managing and playback of podcasts with a few simple commands:

2. 1 Subscription and Discovery:

To subscribe to new podcasts or find interesting episodes, you can ask Siri:
- "Subscribe to [podcast name]. "
- "Search for [podcast genre]. "
- "Find episodes about [topic]. "

2. 2 Playback Controls and Managing Episodes:

Once you discover a podcast you want to listen to, Siri allows you to control playback and manage your podcast library. Here are some useful commands:
- "Play the latest episode of [podcast name]. "
- "Resume my podcast. "
- "Fast forward [x] minutes. "
- "Subscribe to [x] from now each week. "
- "Mark this episode as played. "

3. Enjoying Audiobooks:

Immerse yourself in beautifully narrated stories and thought-provoking non-fiction with audiobooks. Siri can assist you in finding, controlling, and discovering fascinating audiobook content:

3. 1 Acquiring Audiobooks:

With Siri, discovering and adding new audiobooks to your collection is effortless. Just tell Siri:
- "Find audiobooks by [author name]. "
- "Search for [genre] audiobooks. "
- "Get audiobooks by [narrator name]. "

3. 2 Playback and Access:

Once you have an audiobook ready, Siri ensures smooth and frictionless playback. Try these voice commands:

- "Play my current audiobook. "
- "Continue my audiobook. "
- "Skip to the next chapter. "
- "Jump back 30 seconds. "
- "What's the author's name. "

4. Exploring Advanced Music, Podcasts, and Audiobook Features:

Beyond the basics, Siri offers several advanced features, enabling you to dive deeper into your audio content:

4. 1 Music Recommendations:

Siri can recommend music based on your personal tastes. Ask Siri:

- "What's a good song to relax to. "
- "Play some early 2000s hits. "

4. 2 Podcast Discovery:

Siri can help you discover new podcasts based on your interests. Try asking:

- "Find educational podcasts. "
- "Recommend true crime podcasts. "

4. 3 Audiobook Management:

To manage your audiobook library effectively, try these Siri commands:

- "Mark this chapter as a favorite. "
- "What are some popular audiobooks. "
- "Play [audiobook name] from the beginning. "

Conclusion:

Harnessing the power of Siri to control and enjoy your music, podcasts, and audiobooks grants you a truly hands-free and immersive audio experience. With the guidance provided in this chapter, you are well-equipped to dive into Apple Siri's vast array of features and make the most out of your audio content. So, sit back, relax, and let Siri be your versatile virtual assistant for all things audio-related.

# 5.2 Discovering Movies, TV Shows, and Trailers

In today's digital age, entertainment has become an integral part of our lives. People constantly seek out movies, TV shows, and trailers that appeal to their interests and provide a dose of escapism. With Apple Siri's advanced capabilities, discovering these sources of amusement has become easier than ever before. Within the context of this chapter, we will delve into the world of entertainment and learn how to utilize Siri's features to uncover engaging movies, TV shows, and trailers.

5.2.1 Getting Exciting Movie Recommendations:

Siri offers a personalized and efficient way to discover movies that align with your tastes. Tap into Siri's movie knowledge by asking questions like, "What are some top-rated movies this month?" or "Which movies have the best reviews?" Additionally, you can specify genres, actors, or directors to refine your search further. For instance, you could say, "Find me action movies directed by Christopher Nolan."

Furthermore, Siri can cater to your specific mood by asking, "Siri, recommend a funny movie" or "Suggest an exciting thriller." Siri will promptly suggest films that match your desired mood, making your movie-watching experience even more enjoyable.

5.2.2 Navigating Through TV Series:

If you find yourself binge-watching TV shows, Siri is here to assist you in keeping up to date with the latest episodes. Simply ask Siri for recommendations based on your preferred genre or simply request for a popular TV series. For instance, you might ask, "Which shows are trending currently?" or "Recommend some science-fiction series." Siri will swiftly provide you with relevant options, allowing you to stay connected to your favourite TV shows effortlessly.

To enhance your TV watching experience, Siri is equipped with a rich database of information. Ask Siri about the cast, release dates, or ratings of a particular show by saying, "Tell me about the show 'Game of Thrones'" or "Who stars in 'Stranger Things'?" Such queries will enable you to gather comprehensive knowledge about TV series and its creators.

5.2.3 Exploring Trailers:

Trailers often hold the power to captivate enthusiasm and build suspense for upcoming movies. Siri plays an essential role in discovering compelling trailers that ignite anticipation within you. By simply asking, "Siri, show me the latest movie trailers," you can feast your eyes on a vast collection of intriguing previews.

If you are interested in a particular film, Siri can provide detailed information about the movie and its trailer. You may ask questions like, "Show me the trailer for 'The Dark Knight Rises'" or "Can you play the latest Avengers movie trailer?" Siri will promptly find and play the trailer for your viewing pleasure.

To expand your horizons within the entertainment industry, you can utilize Siri in an educational manner as well. By asking Siri about documentaries on specific topics, you can uncover engaging and educational content that ranges from wildlife to history, science, and beyond.

Siri goes beyond serving as a simple search assistant; it aims to cater to your specific needs, preferences, and interests. As you explore movies, TV shows, and trailers with Siri's guidance, you may find hidden gems worth uncovering. Have fun discovering new and exciting entertainment options with the power of Apple Siri at your fingertips!

In conclusion, the entertainment industry offers an abundance of films, TV shows, and trailers to captivate individuals worldwide. Apple Siri, with its intelligent capabilities, serves as an indispensable tool in exploring the vast realm of entertainment. By seamlessly integrating Siri into your search for movies, TV shows, and trailers, you can embark on an exciting journey of discoveries tailored to your preferences and interests. So go ahead, let Siri be your guide, and immerse yourself in the fascinating world of entertainment. Happy exploring!

# 5.3 Sports Scores, News Updates, and Weather Reports

Sports Scores, News Updates, and Weather Reports

Among this day and age, staying updated with the latest sports scores, news updates, and weather reports has become exponentially easier, thanks to the advent of virtual personal assistants like Apple Siri. Siri, integrated into Apple devices and available at your fingertips, allows you to access up-to-date information without lifting a finger. Whether you're a sports enthusiast seeking timely scores, a news junkie hungry for the latest headlines, or a weather follower who likes to plan outings accordingly, Siri has got your back. Among this chapter, we'll explore how Siri can become your go-to option for all things related to sports, news, and even weather reports by delving into its features, command prompts, and different services available.

Let's start with sports scores, shall we? The world of sports can be fast-paced and exhilarating, and staying in the know is crucial for every fan. With Siri, you have an expert companion at your disposal, ready to provide you with updated scores, game schedules, player stats, and much more. To get the latest sports scores, simply activate Siri by holding down the Home button on your Apple device or using a voice-command prompt like "Hey Siri" if your device supports it. Once Siri is activated, you can say something like, "What was the score of last night's game between the Lakers and the Bulls?" Siri will promptly search the web and deliver the most recent score right to your screen, ensuring you never miss a beat. Moreover, Siri can keep you informed about upcoming games, starting times, and even remind you when a match is about to begin, so you can prepare your snacks and cozy up for the action.

Moving on to news updates, Siri can be your personal news anchor, keeping you in the loop with tailored content based on your preferences. Imagine getting a morning briefing with the top stories from your chosen news outlets, just by asking Siri on your Apple device. Whether you're interested in politics, technology, entertainment, or any other topic under the sun, Siri can fetch the latest headlines, summaries, and even full news articles for you. To access news updates, you can ask a variety of questions or give specific commands to Siri, such as, "What are the top news stories of the day?" or "Tell me the latest on climate change." Siri will utilize its impressive search capabilities to comb through a wide range of news sources, ensuring you receive an unbiased view of current events from multiple perspectives.

Weather reports are another essential aspect of staying prepared and making informed decisions. Luckily, Siri has mastered the art of forecasting the weather, so you can plan your outdoor activities seamlessly. With Siri's help, you can effortlessly find out the current temperature, wind speed, humidity, and even a detailed hourly or weekly forecast for any location. Simply ask Siri questions like, "What is the weather like today?" or perhaps be more specific, saying, "Will it rain in New York tomorrow?" Siri will promptly retrieve accurate and timely weather information, helping you dress accordingly and make the most of your day while avoiding unexpected showers or extreme temperatures.

One remarkable feature of Siri is its integration with popular sports, news, and weather apps. Siri harnesses the power of these apps, aggregating the best and most relevant content, ensuring you have access to a vast range of reliable sources at all times. If you prefer a certain sports app or news outlet, you can customize Siri to fetch information from your chosen sources. This way, you can ensure you receive information that aligns with your personal preferences and sources you trust. The customization possibilities offered by Siri allow you to tailor your information consumption to a tee, creating a uniquely personalized experience unmatched by manual searching methods.

It is important to bear in mind that Siri's services may vary depending on contingent factors such as geographical location, language settings, and the version of the operating system on your Apple device. Additionally, Siri's capabilities constantly evolve and improve through software updates, ensuring you get the best possible user experience. Remaining vigilant about updating your device's software will enable you to take advantage of the latest additions and enhancements Siri has to offer when it comes to sports scores, news updates, and weather reports.

In summary, Siri is an intelligent assistant that simplifies and enhances your access to sports scores, news updates, and weather reports. With Siri, you can effortlessly stay informed about the latest scores of your favorite sports teams, get up-to-date news from a wide range of sources, and fine-tune your outdoor plans by receiving detailed weather reports. Siri's integration with popular sports, news, and weather apps provides you with the opportunity to tailor your information intake to your personal preferences. So, go ahead, embrace Siri, and let it become your reliable companion on your journey to becoming a sports aficionado, a well-informed individual, and a weather-savvy planner.

# Chapter 6: Siri Shortcuts and Automation

E ntailed within this chapter, we will dive into the realm of Siri Shortcuts and automation, taking your Siri experience to the next level. Siri Shortcuts and automation allow you to create custom voice commands and automate actions on your Apple devices. With Siri Shortcuts, you can build a personalized collection of tasks that Siri can perform for you, making your daily activities more efficient and streamlined. Automation takes it even further by allowing you to automate various actions triggered by specific events or at certain times. Let's explore how to get started with Siri Shortcuts and automation.

1. Getting acquainted with Siri Shortcuts:

- Open the Shortcuts app on your device (it comes pre-installed with iOS 13 and later versions).

- Tap on "Gallery" to explore pre-made shortcuts or "My Shortcuts" to create your own.

- To create a new shortcut, tap on the "+" button, choose "Create Shortcut," and select actions from the list.

- You can also search for specific actions using the search bar, or browse through different categories.

2. Creating your first Siri Shortcut:

- Tap on the "+" button and select "Create Shortcut."

- Choose the actions you want your shortcut to perform by tapping on each action and configuring its parameters if necessary.

- Once you've added all the actions, tap on the ellipsis (...) button to name your shortcut and add an optional icon.

- Tap on "Done" to save your shortcut, and it will be available in the Shortcuts app and accessible through Siri.

3. Running your Siri Shortcuts:

- To run a shortcut, you can open the Shortcuts app and tap on the shortcut you want to execute.

- Alternatively, you can easily trigger the shortcut with Siri, by saying the phrase you set up while creating the shortcut.

4. Managing your Siri Shortcuts:

- To personalize your shortcuts further, swipe left on a shortcut in "My Shortcuts" and tap on the settings (gear) icon to customize options.

- You can configure parameters like input variables, ask for input, or set up conditional steps.

- Enable "Add to Siri" to assign a custom phrase that will trigger your shortcut.

- Tap on "Share Sheet" to share your shortcut with others or export it to other devices.

5. Exploring advanced Siri Shortcuts features:

- Use parameters like "Repeat with Each" or "If" conditions to enhance the capabilities of your shortcuts.

- Integrate with third-party apps by using their built-in shortcuts or actions.

- Leverage tools like "Text" to interact with text-based inputs or outputs within your shortcut.

- Utilize variables, dictionaries, and magic variables to store and utilize information during the execution of your shortcuts.

6. Automation with Siri and Shortcuts:

- Open the Shortcuts app and switch to the "Automation" tab.

- Tap on the "+" button to create a personal automation or use suggested automations based on your device activity.

- Choose a trigger for the automation, such as time of day, arrival at a specific location, or changes to your device.

- Configure the actions you want to automate, just like you did for Siri Shortcuts.

- Tap on "Next" and review your automation settings before enabling it.

7. Using combined shortcuts and automation:

- Combine Siri Shortcuts with automation to create powerful workflows tailored to your specific needs.

- For example, you can automate the process of preparing for your morning commute using a customized Siri Shortcut triggered by an alarm.

- Another example could be automating a series of actions when arriving home, like turning on the lights, playing your favorite playlist, and adjusting the thermostat.

8. Sharing and discovering Siri Shortcuts and automations:

- Let's not forget about the incredible community of users who create and share their shortcuts.

- Browsing the internet, you'll find various platforms and websites where enthusiasts share their creative shortcuts.

- Feel free to explore and even import these shortcuts to try and modify them to better suit your needs.

With Siri Shortcuts and automation, you hold the power to make your Apple devices adapt to your unique requirements, providing you with a seamless and personalized experience. From automating repetitive tasks to creating complex workflows, Siri becomes your virtual assistant with extraordinary skills. The possibilities are endless as you explore and experiment with the world of Siri Shortcuts and automation. Let your imagination run wild, and let Siri do the heavy lifting for you.

# 6.1 Understanding Siri Shortcuts

6. 1 Understanding Siri Shortcuts

6 Encompassed within this section, we will delve into the fascinating world of Siri Shortcuts. Siri Shortcuts is a powerful feature introduced by Apple that allows users to create custom voice commands to perform specific tasks or automate routine actions on their devices. It provides a seamless integration of artificial intelligence and user customization, empowering individuals to personalize their Siri experience like never before.

To fully grasp the potential behind Siri Shortcuts, it is essential to understand a few key concepts. Let's start by defining what Siri Shortcuts actually are. These shortcuts, as the name implies, serve as condensed versions of complex or lengthy commands that can be triggered with a single voice prompt or a tap.

Through Siri Shortcuts, users can add their favorite commands and actions to the Siri interface and invoke them at any time. You can think of Siri Shortcuts as a bridge between Siri's intelligence and the user's personal preferences. It brings together the convenience of Siri's voice recognition capabilities with the power of customization, creating a unique and personalized user experience.

Now, let us delve deeper into how Siri Shortcuts work. Siri Shortcuts are built upon app-based workflows, allowing various apps to connect and integrate seamlessly within the Siri ecosystem. Developers can add Siri Shortcut support to their apps, enabling users to create custom voice commands or Siri suggestions related to those apps.

To create a Siri Shortcut, you start by selecting an action or a series of actions within a specific app. These actions could range from basic tasks, such as sending a message or playing a specific song, to more complex operations, like setting up a location-based reminder. Once you have chosen the desired actions, you can assign a custom voice command that will trigger the Siri Shortcut. This voice command can be as simple as saying, "Hey Siri, send a message," or as personalized as "Hey Siri, tell my spouse that I will be home soon. "

Siri Shortcuts go beyond simple app-specific actions; they also enable interactions between multiple apps. With this feature, you can connect different apps to create more intricate commands and automate various tasks simultaneously. For example, you might set up a Siri Shortcut that opens your preferred weather app, extracts the current temperature, and automatically sends it to a friend via a messaging app with a personalized message. Through this integration, Siri Shortcuts become powerful tools to streamline your daily routines and enhance your productivity.

In addition to app-based workflows, Apple has also integrated a Suggestions feature within Siri Shortcuts. Suggestions are context-aware shortcuts suggested by Siri based on your usage patterns. These suggestions appear proactively on the Siri watch face, Lock Screen, or the app switcher menu, providing quick and relevant shortcuts based on your typical behaviors and routines. By leveraging this feature, Siri anticipates your needs and assists you with time-saving actions before you even ask. The Shortcuts app allows users to create highly customizable workflows, called shortcuts, using a visual editor. These workflows involve a series of actions and conditions that can be combined and triggered with a custom Siri voice command or manually from the Shortcuts app itself.

The Shortcuts app introduces an extensive array of pre-built automations called Gallery shortcuts, created by both Apple and third-party developers. These shortcuts cover a broad spectrum of functions and serve as inspiring templates for users to modify and adapt to their specific needs. Whether you want to automate your morning routine, control your smart home devices, or streamline your workflow, the Shortcuts app provides an avenue to do it all.

With its user-friendly interface and robust capabilities, Siri Shortcuts open up immense possibilities and empower users to redefine how they interact with their Apple devices. From automating basic tasks to creating complex workflows, Siri Shortcuts serve as a conduit for taking control of your device's capabilities with just a few taps or a command.

In conclusion, Siri Shortcuts offer an exciting opportunity to revolutionize your Siri experience. They bring together the power of customization, artificial intelligence, and seamless integration between apps to provide a truly personalized, efficient, and intuitive user experience. By understanding and harnessing the potential of Siri Shortcuts, you can unlock a world of possibilities and make the most of your Apple Siri experience.

# 6.2 Creating and Customizing Shortcuts

C reating and Customizing Shortcuts
Amidst the pages of this chapter, we will explore one of the most powerful and exciting features of Apple Siri – the ability to create and customize shortcuts. Shortcuts allow you to automate various tasks on your iOS device, making your life easier and more efficient. Whether you want to quickly send a message to a specific contact, set up a routine for your morning commute, or simply automate common actions, Siri Shortcuts can be your reliable companion. Let's delve into the world of Siri Shortcuts and learn how to create and customize them.

Getting Started with Siri Shortcuts

Before we embark on our journey of creating and customizing shortcuts, it is vital to understand the fundamental concepts of Siri Shortcuts. A shortcut is essentially a sequence of actions that Siri carries out when you activate it with a voice command or tap. Think of it as a mini-program that executes specific tasks you define. These tasks can range from basic actions like sending an email or texting someone to more complex operations like combining multiple actions into a single voice command.

Creating Your First Siri Shortcut

To create your first Siri shortcut, follow these simple steps:

1. Launch the Shortcuts app on your iOS device. If you don't have it installed, you can download it for free from the App Store.

2. Tap on the "+" symbol in the top-right corner to create a new shortcut.

3. You will be presented with various recommended shortcuts based on your device usage. You can explore these suggestions, but for now, let's create a custom shortcut. Tap "Create Shortcut."

4. Next, you will enter the editing screen, where you can start building your custom shortcut. Tap on the blue "+" symbol to add an action.

5. You will now have options to select from a list of categories representing different app and system actions. You can customize your shortcut by chaining

multiple actions together. For example, you can start by selecting the Messages app category and then choose the "Send Message" action. Customize the details such as message recipient and content. Once you finish configuring the action, tap "Next."

6. You can name your shortcut by tapping on the "Add Name" field and entering a descriptive name.

7. Choose an icon for your shortcut, making it visually distinguishable. This step is optional, but it can help you quickly identify your shortcuts.

8. Tap "Add to Siri" to set up the voice command that triggers the shortcut. Speak the custom phrase you wish to use, ensuring it's something intuitive and easy to remember. Siri will automatically suggest a phrase based on the shortcut's name.

9. Finally, tap "Done" to create your shortcut.

Customizing Siri Shortcuts

Creating a basic shortcut is a fantastic start, but let's explore the customization options to truly enhance your Siri experience.

1. Open the Shortcuts app and select the shortcut you want to modify.

2. Click on the 3-dot icon in the top-right corner of the shortcut's editing screen.

3. You will see a range of customization options. For example, you can change the icon, reassign the voice command, enable or disable the "Show When Run" switch to determine if the shortcut interface pops up upon execution. You can also make changes to the shortcut configuration by tapping on the blue "+" symbol and editing existing actions or adding new ones.

4. Additionally, you can share your shortcuts with friends or download popular shortcuts shared by the Shortcuts community. Tap on the "More" icon (three dots in a circle) at the bottom-right corner of the shortcut's editing screen, select "Share Shortcut," and explore different sharing options.

Automating Workflows with Siri Shortcuts

Creating a series of actions within a shortcut opens up limitless possibilities to automate numerous workflows throughout your daily routine. With Siri Shortcuts, you can integrate and communicate with various apps on your device, allowing for seamless automation.

Let's take an example of automating your morning routine. Picture this – your alarm rings, and after hitting the snooze button, Siri welcomes you with,

"Good morning! Would you like me to play your favorite morning playlist?". You simply respond with a positive confirmation, and Siri proceeds to cue your favorite music from the Music app. Additionally, Siri automatically adjusts your smart thermostat to your preferred temperature, informs you about current weather conditions, and opens your meditation app.

By combining different actions into a single shortcut, you can create personalized routines that cater to your needs and make your mornings much smoother.

Conclusion

With Siri Shortcuts, Apple equips users with an incredible tool to step into the world of personalized automation. You can create shortcuts for various tasks, customize them to your liking, and incorporate them into your daily life. The possibilities are virtually limitless, and with a little exploration, you will be amazed at how Siri Shortcuts can transform your iOS device into a powerful assistant that simplifies and enriches your experience. So, go ahead, create, and customize your shortcuts, and let Siri enhance your productivity and efficiency like never before.

# 6.3 Automation with Siri and HomeKit Integration

Once you've explored the basics of Apple Siri, it's time to take your interaction with this smart assistant to the next level - automation. Within the context of this chapter, we will dive into the world of Siri and HomeKit integration, allowing you to control various smart home devices with just your voice. Whether you want to unlock the door for your guests, turn off the lights before bed, or adjust the thermostat without leaving your cozy couch, Siri and HomeKit are here to make it happen.

6.3.1 Exploring HomeKit-Compatible Devices

Before delving into automation, it is important to note that not all smart home devices are compatible with HomeKit. HomeKit is Apple's proprietary platform built for seamlessly integrating various smart devices within your household. To utilize Siri's automation capabilities with your smart devices, ensure they are HomeKit-enabled or compatible.

To explore HomeKit-compatible devices, start by opening the Home app on your iOS device. Here, you will discover a wide range of device categories, including lights, outlets, thermostats, locks, and more. Additionally, many third-party apps offer HomeKit device integration, broadly expanding the available options to suit your needs.

6.3.2 Setting Up HomeKit Integration

To begin harnessing Siri's automation powers, open the Home app on your iPhone or iPad and make sure you are signed in with the same Apple ID that you use for Siri. If prompted, follow the on-screen instructions to set up your home in the app. You can assign rooms and designate devices within them for easier control.

Next, install any corresponding apps for the HomeKit-compatible devices you own. These apps usually help with the initial setup, firmware updates, advanced configuration options, and additional features specific to the devices.

Once installed, follow the provided instructions to connect and synchronize the devices with your HomeKit system.

Upon successfully setting up your HomeKit devices, they will automatically become accessible and controllable via the Home app as well as Siri. Remember that each device should have a unique name to avoid confusion and allow both Siri and Home app control.

### 6.3.3 Harnessing Automation Powers with Siri

With your HomeKit devices ready to go, it's time to automate your smart home using Siri's powerful voice commands. Siri's automation capabilities are vast, allowing you to create custom scenes, routines, time-based triggers, and personalized shortcuts. Let's explore each of these to unleash the full potential of Siri and HomeKit integration.

- Custom Scenes: A scene is a preset combination of actions that can be triggered with a single command, enabling you to control multiple devices simultaneously. For example, you can create a "Movie Night" scene that turns off the lights, closes the blinds, and dims the living room lights. To create a scene, open the Home app, tap the "+" icon in the top-right corner, and select "Add Scene." Follow the on-screen instructions to assign actions to your scene and give it a memorable name.

- Routines: Routines build upon scenes by offering additional flexibility and customization. With routines, you can automate actions at specific times or when a certain condition is met. For example, you can set up a "Good Morning" routine that turns on the coffee machine, opens the blinds, and adjusts the thermostat every morning at 7 a.m. To create a routine, open the Home app, tap the "+" icon, select "Automation," and then choose "A Time of Day Occurs" or "A Sensor Detects Something." Configure your personalized routine and assign it a distinct name.

- Time-based Triggers: Time-based triggers allow you to schedule specific actions to occur at precise moments. Whether it's turning off the lights after leaving the house or adjusting the temperature before you return, Siri can ensure everything is just right. To set up a time-based trigger, open the Home app, tap the "+" icon, select "Automation," and then choose "Turn Off" or "Turn On" under "An Accessory is Controlled." Set the desired action, time, and days of the week accordingly.

- Personalized Shortcuts: Siri supports advanced shortcuts, which enable you to utilize multiple actions from various apps in conjunction with HomeKit accessories. Using the Shortcuts app, you can create complex routines that include personalized phrases, automatic actions, and even end-to-end automation across different apps. To create personalized shortcuts, open the Shortcuts app, tap the "+" icon in the top-right corner, and follow the provided instructions to configure your desired commands.

6.3.4 Voice Commands for Automation

Now that you've set up your automated scenes, routines, time-based triggers, and personalized shortcuts, it's time to unleash Siri's automation powers with your voice. Here are some examples of how you can utilize Siri's voice commands for automation:

- "Hey Siri, activate 'Good Morning' routine": Initiates the actions defined in your morning routine, such as turning on the coffee machine and adjusting the thermostat.

- "Hey Siri, turn on the 'Movie Night' scene": Activates the pre-configured scene that dims the lights, closes the blinds, and sets a cozy atmosphere for your movie night.

- "Hey Siri, set the temperature to 72 degrees": Adjusts the thermostat to your desired temperature setting.

- "Hey Siri, turn off the lights in the living room": Deactivates the lights in the specified room.

6.3.5 Troubleshooting and Tips

As with any technological integration, occasionally issues may arise. Here are a few tips and troubleshooting measures to mitigate these:

- Ensure your devices are fully updated with the latest firmware and software versions provided by their respective manufacturers.

- Double-check your device connections and confirm they are connected to the same Wi-Fi network as your iOS device.

- Restart your HomeKit-enabled devices and iOS devices if you encounter any connection or control issues.

- Consider placing Apple TV, HomePod, or iPad within range of your smart home devices to act as a centralized hub, strengthening the system's connectivity.

- Familiarize yourself with your device manufacturer's support resources or reach out to their customer support if you experience persistent or technical issues.

Upgrading your home ecosystem using Siri and HomeKit integration can deliver an unparalleled level of convenience and automation. With an array of compatible devices, limitless customization, and the power of your voice, you can transform your daily routines effortlessly. Unleash Siri's automation capabilities, experiment, and enjoy the wonders of a seamlessly connected and intelligently automated smart home.

# Chapter 7: Advanced Siri Techniques

1. Encompassed within this chapter, we will explore some powerful techniques and features that will help you make the most out of Siri.

2. Creating Custom Siri Shortcuts

- Siri Shortcuts allow you to create personalized voice commands for complex tasks. Learn how to create and manage your own custom shortcuts by leveraging the power of apps that support Siri integration.

- Launch the Shortcuts app and understand its interface.

- Explore the pre-existing actions available in the Shortcuts app and learn how to combine them to create custom shortcuts.

- Customize the invocation phrase for your shortcuts for ease of use.

- Import and export shortcuts to share them with other users.

- Discover handy shortcuts created by other users and download them for your daily use.

3. Mastering Siri Suggestions and Proactive Assistance

- Siri Suggestions and Proactive Assistance make Siri proactive by trying to anticipate your needs and actions. Understand how this feature works and how to get the most out of it.

- Configure Siri Suggestions preferences to enable or disable specific app suggestions.

- Learn how Siri adapts to your habits and behavior over time to provide tailored suggestions.

- Utilize Siri Watch Face on your Apple Watch to display contextual information and recommendations throughout the day.

- Understand how Siri leverages contextual information to suggest actions based on your location, time, and previous activities.

- Explore advanced Siri Suggestions settings to manage privacy concerns and control the content Siri can access.

4. Controlling Your Home with Siri and HomeKit

- Siri can become your smart home coordinator by controlling HomeKit-compatible devices with just your voice. Discover how to set up and control your smart home automation.

- Get to know the Home app and understand its features.

- Connect and configure various HomeKit-enabled devices like lights, thermostats, cameras, and speakers.

- Control individual devices or sets of devices with Siri voice commands.

- Set up scenes to control multiple devices simultaneously with a single voice command.

- Automate your smart home by using triggers and conditions in the Home app.

5. Fine-Tuning Siri's Voice Recognition

- Siri heavily relies on voice recognition to accurately understand and execute your commands. Learn how to improve Siri's voice recognition and reduce errors.

- Train Siri to recognize your voice by completing the voice training process.

- Practice speaking clearly and enunciating words to enhance Siri's accuracy.

- Understand the impact of background noise on voice recognition and learn strategies to minimize it.

- Discover how to modify your queries or commands to increase comprehension.

6. Leveraging Siri's Multilingual and Translation Capabilities

- Siri supports multiple languages and can even help you with translations. Unlock Siri's multilingual capabilities by enabling new languages and exploring its translation capabilities.

- Add additional languages to Siri and switch between them effortlessly.

- Learn how to ask Siri to translate specific words, phrases, or sentences.

- Understand which languages are supported for translation and what to expect from Siri's translation capabilities.

- Use Siri to practice pronunciation of words in different languages.

7. Advanced Siri Settings and Personalization

- Dive deeper into Siri's settings to further tailor it to your preferences and enhance your overall user experience.

- Customize Siri's voice and accent by selecting from various available options.
- Fine-tune the Siri voice activation settings to optimize Siri's responsiveness to your commands.
- Explore the settings related to Siri's compatibility with the Lock screen and adjust it to your liking.
- Utilize additional accessibility options to enhance Siri's usability for users with specific needs.
- Familiarize yourself with Siri's voice feedback options and adapt them to your preferences.

8. Solving Common Problems and Misunderstandings

- Sometimes Siri might not fully understand or execute your commands as expected. Learn some troubleshooting techniques to overcome common issues and get back on track.
- Identify common reasons for misinterpretation and learn how to rephrase your commands for successful execution.
- Troubleshoot common connection issues that may prevent Siri from functioning properly.
- Resolve issues related to Siri Suggestions not appearing or inaccurate.
- Discover strategies to address potential privacy concerns associated with using Siri.

9. Future Prospects of Siri and Emerging Technologies

- Siri continues to evolve with every iOS update and integrate with new technologies. Gain insight into promising developments and potential future use cases of Siri.
- Understand how Siri integrates with machine learning and improves its capabilities over time.
- Explore potential advancements in natural language processing and conversational AI that may benefit Siri.
- Discover the role of Siri in Apple's ecosystem, including its interactions with new devices and services as they become available.
- Speculate on future use cases for Siri, such as supporting augmented reality experiences or expanding its capabilities in different domains.

10. You are now equipped with advanced techniques to unlock the full potential of Siri's voice-enabled assistance and automation capabilities. Enjoy

interacting with Siri and discovering new ways to enhance your productivity, control your smart home, and access valuable information with just your voice. Remember, Siri is constantly improving, so stay updated with new releases and enjoy the ongoing evolution of this powerful AI assistant.

# 7.1 Advanced Voice Commands and Queries

A mong this section, we will dive deeper into the realm of Siri's advanced voice commands and queries. These features allow you to perform a wide range of tasks with greater efficiency and control. By mastering these techniques, you can harness the full potential of Siri and make your everyday life easier.

1. Workflow Automation:

One of the most powerful features of Siri is its ability to automate workflows. By creating custom shortcuts, you can combine multiple actions into a single voice command. For example, you can set up a shortcut that turns off your lights, adjusts the thermostat, and plays your favorite music by simply saying a specific phrase. You can explore and create your own shortcuts through the Siri Shortcuts app.

2. HomeKit Integration:

If you have a smart home setup, you can use Siri to control various devices and appliances. Through Siri's integration with Apple's HomeKit, you can turn on/off lights, adjust the temperature, lock doors, and much more by just using your voice. You can set up scenes to automate multiple actions simultaneously, such as having Siri prepare your home for bedtime or a movie night.

3. Media Control:

Siri allows you to control media playback on your iPhone, iPad, Apple TV, or other supported devices. You can ask Siri to play a specific song, album, or playlist from your music library or streaming services like Apple Music. Additionally, Siri can pause, resume, skip, or shuffle your content. You can even request Siri to play music on specific AirPlay-compatible speakers or multi-room audio systems.

4. App-Specific Commands:

Siri supports a wide range of apps and can help you perform various tasks within them. For example, you can ask Siri to send a message on WhatsApp or WeChat, make a reservation on OpenTable, call a ride through Uber or

Lyft, or even order food from your favorite delivery app. It's worth exploring Siri's compatibility with the apps you regularly use and discovering the specific commands that apply to each one.

5. Find and Search:

Siri can also assist you in finding information quickly and effortlessly. For instance, you can ask Siri to locate nearby restaurants, find the movie showtimes in your area, check sports scores, or search for specific files, emails, or messages on your device. Siri can search the web, Wikipedia, and other sources to provide you with the information you need.

6. Advanced Web Commands:

Additionally, Siri provides advanced web commands that enable you to perform web searches, add events to your calendar, and create reminders. Siri can help you search for information using specific search engines, book flights, check the status of your flights, send emails, or create notes. These advanced web commands make Siri an invaluable personal assistant for your digital life.

7. Accessibility Features:

Finally, Siri includes various accessibility features that cater to users with specific needs. These features allow individuals with physical disabilities or impairments to interact with their devices more effectively. For example, Siri provides options for voice dictation, voice control, voice recognition customization, and more. These features open up a world of opportunities for users who may require alternative input methods.

By familiarizing yourself with these advanced voice commands and queries, you can enhance your Siri experience and leverage the full potential of this powerful virtual assistant. Whether it's automating your workflows, controlling your smart home devices, or searching for information, Siri is designed to make your life more convenient and connected. So, don't hesitate to explore and experiment with all the possibilities Siri brings to your fingertips.

# 7.2 Multi-Language Support and Translation

One of the remarkable features of Apple Siri is its extensive multi-language support and translation capabilities. Siri is designed to provide users with assistance in various languages, making it accessible for people from diverse linguistic backgrounds.

When it comes to multi-language support, Siri boasts an impressive range of over forty languages. This means that Siri can understand and respond to queries not just in English but also in languages like Spanish, French, Mandarin, German, Arabic, and many more. This multi-language support reflects the global nature of Siri's user base and Apple's commitment to inclusivity.

To ensure Siri understands your preferred language, you can easily set your desired language and region settings on your Apple device. Once configured, Siri will automatically use those settings to adapt its responses and provide a seamless and personalized experience.

Now, let's delve into the translation capabilities of Siri. If you find yourself in a situation where you need to communicate with someone who speaks a different language, Siri can be a valuable tool. Siri acts as an instant translator, allowing you to convert your phrases or sentences from one language to another.

To use Siri for translation, simply ask it to translate a particular phrase or ask for a translation of a specific word. For instance, you can say, "Translate 'hello' to Spanish," and Siri will quickly respond with the corresponding Spanish translation, "hola." This functionality can prove incredibly useful while traveling or even in day-to-day conversations with people who speak different languages.

Furthermore, Siri's translation capabilities aren't limited to a one-way street. You can also further the conversation by saying, "And now translate 'how are you?' back to English." Siri will effortlessly translate your query back to English, enabling a natural and engaging conversation with individuals speaking other languages.

What's especially fascinating about Siri's translation feature is its ability to handle context. Siri doesn't merely provide literal translations; it also takes into account the meaning and intent behind your phrases. This contextual understanding allows it to generate accurate translations that feel human-like and ensure effective communication between individuals speaking different languages.

Additionally, Apple continually enhances Siri's translation capabilities by utilizing advanced machine learning algorithms. By leveraging vast amounts of language data, Siri improves its translation accuracy and continues to evolve over time. This means that Siri's translations become more refined, accurate, and natural with each update, ensuring an ever-improving user experience.

In conclusion, Siri's multi-language support and translation capabilities demonstrate Apple's commitment to making technology accessible and inclusive for people from different linguistic backgrounds. Whether you need assistance in various languages or want to bridge language barriers while conversing with others, Siri proves to be an invaluable asset. Moreover, as Apple continues to iterate on Siri's translation features through machine learning advancements, users can expect even more accurate and intuitive translations in the future. So, embrace Siri's linguistic prowess and embark on a journey towards global communication without limitations.

# 7.3 Siri's Integration with Third-Party Apps

In recent years, Apple has been dedicated to expanding the capabilities of Siri by integrating it with third-party apps. This integration has significantly enhanced the usefulness and versatility of Siri, offering users a seamless experience across various applications. Among this section, we will explore the advantages of Siri's integration with third-party apps and how it can make your life easier.

One of the crucial benefits of Siri's integration with third-party apps is the ability to perform tasks hands-free. Instead of fiddling with your iPhone or iPad, you can now simply ask Siri to execute specific commands in supported third-party apps. For instance, while driving, you can say, "Hey Siri, send a message to John on WhatsApp, saying I'll be there in 15 minutes." Siri will take care of sending the message without requiring you to take your eyes off the road.

Additionally, third-party app integration expands Siri's knowledge base and gives it access to a broader range of information. Prior to this integration, Siri relied on native iOS applications for executing tasks and retrieving information. However, with third-party apps, Siri gains the capability to access information and functionalities beyond its native boundaries. This integration enables Siri to provide more precise and comprehensive responses to your queries.

Siri's integration with third-party apps also greatly improves task automation and streamlines your workflow. By allowing Siri to interact with your favorite third-party apps, you can perform complex actions with ease. For instance, you can say, "Hey Siri, order groceries from Instacart and set a reminder to pay the bill on 'Due' app." Siri will seamlessly connect and coordinate with these third-party apps, ensuring that your tasks are executed efficiently and promptly.

Furthermore, Siri's integration with third-party apps brings voice-first control to a wide array of services and utilities. Initially only limited to Apple's own ecosystem, Siri now extends its capabilities to an ever-growing list of external developers. This means that you can perform a variety of actions using voice commands, such as sending money through PayPal, booking flights and hotels through Expedia, or ordering food through delivery apps like Uber Eats or Postmates. With Siri, the possibilities are nearly endless.

To take advantage of Siri's integration with third-party apps, ensure that you have the latest version of iOS installed on your device. Developers of third-party apps often release updates to add Siri compatibility and enhance the overall user experience. By keeping your apps up to date, you'll be able to take full advantage of the latest Siri features and integrations.

In conclusion, Siri's integration with third-party apps has revolutionized the way we interact with our devices. It offers a hands-free, seamless experience that enhances productivity and efficiency. With the ability to interact with a growing number of third-party apps, Siri becomes an indispensable tool for managing tasks, accessing information, and automating various processes in your daily life. So go ahead, experiment with Siri and explore the myriad of possibilities it opens up for you.

# Chapter 8: Privacy and Security

In an age where digital privacy and security are increasingly valued, staying informed about how Siri handles your personal data and understanding the measures taken to protect your information is crucial. Apple is committed to maintaining the privacy and security of Siri users, and in this chapter, we will delve into the various aspects related to privacy and security in regard to Siri.

1. Why Is Privacy Important?

Privacy is not merely a matter of confidentiality; it is a fundamental human right. With advancements in technology, our digital footprint grows larger every day, making it essential to ensure our information remains secure. For Siri, privacy involves safeguarding your data from unauthorized access while upholding stringent measures for responsible data handling.

2. How Does Siri Protect Your Privacy?

When you use Siri, it is designed to respect your privacy by only uploading data in an anonymous and encrypted format. Apple follows a series of practices to protect your privacy:

i. Data Minimization: Siri processes your requests without attaching any personally identifiable information (PII) to it. Any data sent to Apple is combined with billions of other queries, making it nearly impossible to trace back to an individual user.

ii. User Control: Apple values user choice, and Siri provides the option to disable or enable its features based on individual preferences. For instance, you can limit Siri access when your device is locked to prevent unintentional activation.

iii. Transparency and Control: The Apple website offers detailed documentation on how your data is handled, including Siri data. Users have access to manage their own data within their accounts, and Apple provides tools to review and delete Siri history, whenever desired.

3. How Does Siri Keep Your Data Secure?

The security of your data while using Siri is of paramount importance to Apple. Here are some security measures implemented by Apple to protect your data:

i. Encryption: All communications between your device and Apple servers are end-to-end encrypted, ensuring that even if intercepted, your data remains private.

ii. On-device Processing: To maintain privacy, as much processing as possible is done right on your device. Siri has the capability to understand and respond to your requests without needing to constantly send data back to Apple servers.

iii. Consent-based Access: Siri requires your explicit consent for access to certain data categories like contacts or location information. The request is shown on your device, underscoring the importance of informed user consent.

4. Apple's Intelligent Tracking Prevention

Beyond Siri, Apple takes privacy seriously across its ecosystem. In Safari, Apple has introduced Intelligent Tracking Prevention, a feature that blocks trackers used by advertisers for targeted marketing. This empowers users to browse the web without worrying about their online activities being excessively monitored or their data being misused.

5. Continual Improvement and Independent Audits

Apple is constantly evaluating and enhancing its privacy protections and practices surrounding Siri. To maintain transparency and reassure users, Apple often undergoes independent security audits to verify compliance with privacy standards. These audits ensure that Apple adheres to its commitment of protecting user privacy.

Conclusion:

Privacy and security are cornerstone considerations in any digital service, and with Siri, Apple has implemented robust measures to safeguard your data. By using features like data minimization, encryption, user control, and on-device processing, Apple has gone above and beyond to ensure Siri respects and protects your privacy. Continued enhancements, such as Intelligent Tracking Prevention and regular independent audits, underscore Apple's commitment to maintaining user trust. With this knowledge, you can confidently embrace Siri and reap the benefits of its assistive capabilities while staying in control of your privacy.

# 8.1 Siri's Data Handling Practices

S iri's Data Handling Practices: Ensuring Privacy and Security in Your
Interactions

ENCLOSED WITHIN THIS chapter, we will delve into the world of Siri
and explore its data handling practices. Siri, Apple's voice-controlled personal
virtual assistant, has revolutionized the way we interact with our devices. But
with its capabilities to personalize responses and suggestions, concerns related
to user privacy and data security naturally arise. Enclosed within this guideline,
we will uncover how Siri handles user data, its commitment to privacy, and the
measures it takes to ensure your information remains secure.

Understanding Siri's Data Collection:

By design, Siri collects certain data to offer personalized experiences and
provide accurate responses. However, Apple is committed to respecting user
privacy and employs strict guidelines in its data collection practices. Siri
generally processes user data on-device, keeping most of the information within
the device's hardware for privacy reasons. Apple prioritizes the user's control
over their data and adopts techniques like differential privacy to anonymize and
protect individuals' information.

On-Device Processing and User Privacy:

One primary aspect that sets Siri apart from other voice assistants is its
on-device processing. Unlike some competitors, Siri performs substantial tasks
offline to safeguard your privacy. When you give voice commands or pose
questions to Siri, it processes your speech and linguistic patterns locally,
reducing the need to send your voice data to external servers. Executing much
of the analysis on the device further limits the exposure of your personal
information to potentially vulnerable networks.

Preventing Unintentional Data Collection:

While Siri requires some amount of user data to function effectively, Apple continually works to reduce the unintentional collection of private information. For instance, when Siri is activated inadvertently, it listens for explicit keywords or phrases before activating fully. Additionally, Apple allows users to easily adjust the Siri settings to grant limited access or disable certain functionalities to suit their comfort level.

Opt-in Data Sharing:

As part of its continued commitment to security and personal privacy, Apple has implemented a policy of opt-in data sharing. This means that, unless you explicitly give consent, Siri does not collect identifiable information that can be linked to you personally. Therefore, Siri's data collection practices remain highly limited and focused on only what is necessary to deliver the desired functionalities.

Differential Privacy: Protecting Your Privacy While Improving Siri:

To improve Siri's speech recognition, natural language processing, and other features, Apple implements a technique called differential privacy. This approach ensures that when Apple collects data to improve Siri's capabilities, the shared information is carefully stripped of personally identifiable elements. By injecting intentionally crafted noise into the data, Apple guarantees privacy while benefiting from collective statistical information to advance Siri's performance.

User Control and Transparency:

Apple prioritizes empowering users with control over their data. With Siri, you can review and control your privacy settings by navigating through your device settings. These settings enable you to manage Siri's access to various aspects like contacts, location, emails, and more. Furthermore, Apple provides transparency reports in which they outline the number and types of requests they may receive from law enforcement agencies concerning user information.

In-App Integration and Data Sharing:

Siri's integration within various applications provides added convenience and functionality. However, it is crucial to be aware of the data sharing practices associated with third-party apps. Apple enforces strict privacy guidelines for developers, prescribing that user permission must be obtained before various types of personal data, such as contacts or photos, can be accessed by Siri within these apps. Always ensure that you review and understand an app's privacy policy before granting permissions to use Siri functionality.

Conclusion:

With Siri becoming increasingly integrated into our daily lives, understanding its data handling practices becomes crucial. Apple's commitment to privacy and security ensures that while Siri leverages user data to offer personalized experiences, it prioritizes protecting individuals' information. By utilizing on-device processing, adopting differential privacy techniques, and granting user control over data access, Siri demonstrates its commitment to ensuring your privacy is respected. So, harness the power of Siri with the confidence that your personal information remains under your control and secure in Apple's ecosystem.

# 8.2 Managing Personal Information and Permissions

A mid this section, we will delve into the topic of managing personal information and permissions in Apple Siri. Protecting your personal data is crucial in this digital age, and Siri offers various settings and options to help you maintain control over your information. We will explore how to manage your personal information, control Siri's access to different data sources, and ensure your privacy is safeguarded.

1. Guarding Your Personal Information:

When using Siri, you might interact with the assistant by asking questions or giving voice commands that disclose personal details. Siri has access to your contacts, messages, emails, and other important data necessary to perform its functions effectively. However, it is vital to stress that Apple emphasizes privacy, and Siri doesn't retain your conversations or associate them with your Apple ID. To maintain this privacy, Apple recommends taking a few steps:

a. Understanding Data Usage: Familiarize yourself with the kind of data Siri can access, including contacts, reminders, calendar events, and more. Knowing this will enable you to control what Siri can utilize to provide you with personalized assistance.

b. Remain Diligent: Siri is designed to respect your privacy, but you should still be cautious while interacting. Avoid dictating sensitive content such as passwords, credit card numbers, or personal identification details that compromise your security.

c. Opting Out: If you decide that you no longer want Siri to access your data, you can disable Siri entirely or disable access to specific sources such as Contacts, Messages, or Calendars from the Siri & Search settings.

2. Managing Permissions and Access:

Siri requires your permission to access certain data sources, and Apple provides enhanced controls to manage these permissions effectively. Here are some primary areas to focus on:

a. Understanding Siri & Search Permissions: Access Siri's permissions via your device's Settings. Navigate to Siri & Search, where you can manage permissions for various apps and data sources. Applications with Siri integration will display their settings here, giving you control over what information Siri can access from each app.

b. Customizing App Access: Control which apps Siri can use on your device by selecting the particular app within Siri & Search settings. You can then toggle on or off the access to specific apps and fine-tune Siri's capabilities.

c. Individual App Settings: Some third-party apps have their own Siri permissions that need to be customized from within the app itself. If you want to grant or revoke Siri's access to a specific application, explore that app's individual settings.

3. Apple ID and iCloud Considerations:

To manage full control over your personal information, ensure you're aware of how Siri interacts with your Apple ID and iCloud account.

a. Apple ID Settings: Within your Apple ID settings, access the "Privacy" option to manage your personal information settings. This area provides fine-grained control over which data Siri can access and use, including Contacts, Calendars, and Emails.

b. iCloud Security: As Siri may use information stored on your iCloud account for better personal productivity, it is crucial to maintain good security practices for your Apple ID and iCloud account. Enabling two-factor authentication, using strong passwords, and periodically reviewing your security settings can ensure the safeguarding of your data.

4. Deleting Siri Data:

At times, you may want Siri to start fresh or remove specific information it has gathered over time. Apple offers options to manage and delete your Siri data promptly.

a. Siri History: You can access your Siri history by going to the Siri & Search settings and selecting "Siri & Dictation History." From there, you have the choice to review your interactions and delete individual requests or clear the entire Siri history.

b. Contacting Apple Support: If you face any concerns about your Siri interactions or require assistance with managing your data, Apple Support is available to provide guidance and resolve any issues.

Conclusion:

By taking the time to manage your personal information and permission settings, you can harness Siri's functionality while ensuring your privacy remains intact. Apple has implemented numerous controls and features to empower users in managing their data effectively. Remember to regularly review your personal settings, deal diligently with sensitive information, and leverage the available resources to fully benefit from the power of Siri while maintaining your privacy and security.

# 8.3 Enhancing Siri's Privacy and Security Settings

Siri, Apple's virtual assistant, has transformed the way we interact with our devices, allowing us to complete tasks and get information simply by using our voice. As Siri has become an integral part of our lives, it is crucial to prioritize the importance of privacy and security settings. Amidst these chapter, we will delve into the various aspects of enhancing Siri's privacy and security settings.

Privacy concerns have become a pressing issue in today's digital age, and Apple is committed to addressing them. With Siri, Apple has implemented robust measures to ensure that user data remains secure and protected. However, it is essential for users to be aware of and make use of these features to safeguard their personal information effectively.

The first step in enhancing Siri's privacy and security settings begins right from the initial setup process. During setup, Apple provides users with the choice to decide whether they want to enable Siri on their device or not. You have complete control over this decision. It is vital to understand that Siri operates by processing voice and audio data in the background. By enabling Siri, you grant permission to Apple to collect and store this data, ensuring Siri functions seamlessly and efficiently.

Apple's commitment to user privacy is further bolstered by its privacy-focused practices. In iOS 14 and later, Apple introduced a new feature called "On-Device Speech Recognition." This feature allows Siri to process your voice requests more locally on your device, without sending them to Apple's servers. By choosing this option, your voice requests are processed on your device alone, mitigating privacy concerns about audio being sent to external servers.

To enable "On-Device Speech Recognition," navigate to Settings on your iOS device. Locate the Siri & Search menu and select Siri & Dictation History. Next, choose the "Delete Siri & Dictation History" option to clear any existing recorded audio. This step ensures that Siri no longer relies on older recordings and instead processes your voice requests exclusively on your device.

In addition to optimizing Siri's voice recognition, Apple has implemented privacy safeguards within Siri's settings. By accessing Siri & Search under the Settings menu, you can customize Siri to your preferences while managing privacy and security concerns. Let's explore some key features that will allow you to enhance Siri's privacy and security configuration.

1. Listen for "Hey Siri": The "Listen for 'Hey Siri'" option lets you activate Siri by merely saying the "Hey Siri" phrase. To ensure private and secure usage, Apple provides an option to train Siri to recognize only your voice and deactivate responding to unrecognized users. To enable this feature, go to the Siri & Search settings and toggle the "Listen for 'Hey Siri'" option. Then, follow the on-screen instructions to train Siri to your voice.

2. Voice Feedback: Siri can provide voice feedback while responding to your requests, assisting you in certain scenarios. However, if privacy is your priority, you have the option to set Siri's responses to work silently. To configure this, go to the Siri & Search menu, select Voice Feedback, and choose the desired option - either Always On, Control with Ring Switch, or Hands-Free Only.

3. Siri Suggestions: Siri provides suggestions based on your device usage patterns to enhance your overall user experience. Some privacy-conscious users may prefer not to utilize this feature due to the personal information it relies upon. You can adjust Siri's suggestions settings under Siri & Search Preferences, where you have control over which apps utilize Siri's suggestions. Simply enable or disable the suggestions for specific apps according to your preferences.

4. Privacy Hub: Apple recognizes that privacy protection requires a comprehensive approach. Therefore, they have introduced the Privacy Hub, easily accessible through Settings. Here, you can find detailed explanations of each privacy setting available for Siri and review your data to ensure your privacy is intact.

5. Location Services: Siri can gather location information to support various requests effectively. If you are concerned about location privacy, you can customize location access permissions for Siri. Under Settings, navigate to Privacy and choose Location Services. Scroll down until you find Siri & Dictation. From there, you can specify whether you permit Siri to access your

location information, allowing for a tailored experience without compromising privacy.

6. Language and Profanity Filters: Siri is equipped with a profanity filter to prevent inappropriate content from being played or displayed on your device. To manage these settings, go to Siri & Search and navigate to the Language menu. Here, you can set your preferred language for Siri, while simultaneously managing restrictions and ensuring a safe and tailored interaction.

7. Third-Party App Access: Siri extends its assistance to certain third-party applications for an enhanced user experience. However, if you value privacy and wish to limit these integrations, you have complete control to manage app access. Under Siri & Search, select the app that you don't want Siri to interact with and toggle off its permission. This empowers you to customize Siri's engagement, ensuring your information remains protected from unnecessary external interactions.

Lastly, it is essential to emphasize that your privacy and security rely not only on device settings but also on your overall online behavior. While Apple takes significant measures to ensure data protection, it is crucial to remain mindful of the information you share and exercise restraint when providing access permissions. Regularly reviewing and updating your device's privacy and security settings will further enhance your peace of mind while using Siri.

By involving the user from the initial setup and offering a multitude of customizable settings covering voice recognition, input preferences, access controls, and diligent information management, Apple empowers users to genuinely enhance the privacy and security aspects of Siri. Making thoughtful decisions while configuring these settings creates an environment where you feel confident and secure while interacting with Siri.

In conclusion, prioritizing privacy and security settings when using Siri is an essential aspect of harnessing the full potential of Apple's virtual assistant. Through configurable choices starting from the device setup and customizable Siri settings, Apple truly grants users control over their data. By thoroughly exploring and implementing these suggested guidelines, beginners can navigate Siri with confidence, ensuring their privacy is preserved while enjoying the convenience and power of this remarkable tool.

# Chapter 9: Troubleshooting and FAQs

Now that you have learned the basics of Apple Siri and have been exploring its features, there may come a time when you encounter certain issues or have questions about its functionality. Entailed within this chapter, we will delve into troubleshooting common problems and understanding frequently asked questions related to Siri. By the end of this chapter, you will be equipped with the knowledge and resources to overcome any obstacles you may face while using Siri.

Section 1: Troubleshooting Siri Issues

1. Siri not responding or working properly:

- Check your internet connection: Siri requires an active internet connection. Ensure that your device is connected to a stable Wi-Fi or cellular network.

- Disable Low Power Mode: When your device is in Low Power Mode, certain features, including Siri, may be limited to conserve battery. Adjust your device settings accordingly.

- Enable Siri: Confirm that Siri is enabled on your device by going to Settings > Siri & Search and toggle the switch to turn it on.

- Reboot your device: Sometimes a simple restart can resolve temporary glitches. To reboot your iPhone, hold down the Sleep/Wake button and slide to power off, then turn the device on again after a few seconds.

2. Misinterpretation or inaccurate responses:

- Speak clearly: Ensure that you are speaking clearly and enunciating words properly to help Siri understand your commands accurately.

- Reduce ambient noise: Background noise can interfere with Siri's ability to comprehend your speech. Move to a quieter location or hold the device closer to your mouth.

- Update iOS and Siri: Keeping your device updated with the latest iOS and Siri version can prevent compatibility issues and improve Siri's performance. Go to Settings > General > Software Update to check for any available updates.

- Train Siri: You can enhance Siri's accuracy by using the voice recognition option in Settings > Siri & Search > My Siri Voice. This feature trains Siri to recognize your voice better.

Section 2: Frequently Asked Questions

Q1: Can I change Siri's voice.

- Yes, you can change Siri's voice. Go to Settings > Siri & Search > Siri Voice, and choose a preferred voice accent and gender. You can also customize Siri's language to match your preference.

Q2: How does Siri handle multiple languages.

- Siri supports multiple languages, and you can switch between them by going to Settings > Siri & Search > Language. However, keep in mind that some features may not be available in all languages.

Q3: Will Siri synchronize across my Apple devices.

- Yes, Siri synchronization is available across all your Apple devices signed in with the same Apple ID. This allows you to seamlessly use Siri on your iPhone, iPad, Mac, Apple Watch, and HomePod, with data and preferences carried over.

Q4: Can Siri control third-party apps.

- Siri can control various third-party apps, but it depends on whether the app developers have integrated their app with Siri's capabilities. Some popular apps like WhatsApp, Spotify, and Uber have Siri integration.

Q5: How secure is Siri in terms of privacy.

- Apple prioritizes user privacy and has implemented measures to protect your data. Siri's voice recognition and processing occur on your device, minimizing the risk of your private information being shared. Apple encrypts Siri-related data when it's sent to their servers and uses it only to improve the service.

Q6: Can I disable Siri on my device.

- Yes, if you decide not to use Siri, you can disable it in the device settings. Go to Settings > Siri & Search and turn off the Siri toggle switch.

Conclusion:

Troubleshooting common Siri issues and addressing frequently asked questions can be crucial in ensuring a smooth Siri experience. Entailed within this chapter, we discussed troubleshooting techniques to address Siri not responding or working properly, as well as tips to improve its accuracy. Additionally, we explored common questions users have regarding voice customization, language support, app integration, privacy, and disabling Siri when desired. Armed with this knowledge, you are now better equipped to navigate Siri effectively and troubleshoot any challenges that may arise.

# 9.1 Common Siri Issues and Solutions

Among this section, we will explore some of the common issues that users might encounter while using Apple Siri and provide effective solutions to overcome them. Siri is an intelligent virtual assistant that requires an internet connection and works seamlessly with various Apple devices such as iPhones, iPads, Macs, and HomePods. However, like any technology, Siri can sometimes face difficulties in understanding commands or delivering accurate responses. Let's dive in and explore how to troubleshoot these common Siri issues.

1. "Hey Siri" Not Working:

One common problem users face is when their device fails to respond to the "Hey Siri" wake-up command. Firstly, ensure that your device supports the "Hey Siri" functionality and that it is properly enabled in the settings. If the feature is enabled and still not working, try restarting your device or resetting Siri's trained voice. You can reset Siri's voice by going to Settings > Siri & Search > Siri Voice, and selecting a different voice. Additionally, ensure that your device isn't in Low Power Mode, as this may disable "Hey Siri" functionality.

2. Siri Misunderstands or Misinterprets Requests:

Siri's primary function is to interpret voice commands accurately. However, in some instances, it may misinterpret or misunderstand the user's requests. To overcome this issue, ensure that you speak clearly and use the appropriate language. Pronounce names and places correctly to enhance Siri's comprehension. If Siri continually misinterprets requests, you can improve voice recognition accuracy by going to Settings > Siri & Search > Language and selecting the preferred language with the best recognition success rate.

3. Siri Fails to Perform Specific Tasks:

Siri possesses numerous capabilities, but there might be times when it fails to perform certain tasks. For instance, if Siri cannot send text messages or make calls, verify that the corresponding permissions are granted and that the contact details are accurately stored in your device's contacts. If Siri has problems accessing other apps or functions, ensure that you have the latest software updates installed.

4. Siri Does Not Read Out Messages:

Siri has a useful feature that reads out new messages when received. If Siri fails to read out messages audibly, make sure that the device's mute switch is not enabled and that the volume is appropriately set. Check if Siri's voice is functioning by asking it simple questions like the current time or day, as this will unveil any issues with audio playback.

5. Siri Cannot Connect to the Internet:

Since Siri's backend functions with an internet connection, it might encounter connectivity issues. If Siri repeatedly fails to connect to the internet, restart your wireless router or switch to a more stable network connection. Additionally, disable and re-enable Siri to reset the connection and ensure that the issue is not related to a system-wide internet outage.

6. Siri Raises Privacy Concerns:

Some individuals may worry about their privacy when using Siri, considering that your conversations are processed by Apple servers. You can alleviate these concerns by reviewing Siri's privacy settings. Open Settings > Siri & Search and check options like "Listen for 'Hey Siri'" and "Allow Siri When Locked" to customize and enhance Siri's privacy settings as per your comfort level.

7. Siri Features Unavailable in Your Region:

Certain Siri features may not be available in all regions or countries. In such cases, you may encounter restrictions on specific queries, services, or dialects. To address this, ensure that your device region settings reflect the region where the Siri function should work optimally. You can check and modify your region settings by going to Settings > General > Language & Region.

While Siri strives to enhance user experience and simplify daily tasks, technical issues can occasionally arise. Troubleshooting common Siri problems, as discussed above, will help you navigate and resolve difficulties effectively. Apple continuously improves Siri's functionality with software updates, so keep an eye out for those updates to benefit from the latest enhancements and bug fixes. Remember to explore Siri's extensive capabilities and enjoy the benefits of having a virtual assistant at your fingertips.

# 9.2 Improving Siri's Recognition and Understanding

Siri, as one of the most popular virtual assistants, has revolutionized the way we interact with our devices. While it offers remarkable features and capabilities, there's always room for improvement, especially when it comes to Siri's recognition and understanding of user commands. Inside this chapter, we aim to explore ways to enhance Siri's performance in recognizing and comprehending our queries.

1. Clarity in Pronunciation:

One common issue that can hinder Siri's accurate recognition is a lack of clarity in pronunciation. To overcome this, it's important to enunciate words clearly and avoid mumbling. Speaking at a moderate pace and eliminating background noise can significantly improve Siri's ability to understand commands accurately. Remember, Siri relies on precise pronunciation to accurately translate voice inputs into actions or searches.

2. Contextual Understanding:

Understanding context is crucial for Siri to provide accurate and relevant responses. Apple has been continually improving Siri's context-awareness, allowing it to better grasp user queries by considering previous conversations or the current application in use. Nevertheless, providing clearer and more detailed information can further enhance Siri's understanding. For instance, instead of saying "message John," saying "text John, 'Let's meet for lunch tomorrow at 1 p.m.'" provides more context for Siri, leading to a more precise outcome.

3. Vocabulary Expansion:

As with any language-based tool, Siri's language comprehension is limited to its programmed vocabulary. Understandably, Siri's vocabulary is vast, but there may be instances where it fails to comprehend domain-specific terms or recent slang. In such cases, users can help enhance Siri's performance by providing alternative or more explicit phrasing. Furthermore, Apple encourages users to provide feedback on any unrecognized terms to accelerate vocabulary expansions in software updates.

4. Accurate Queries:

To improve Siri's understanding, it's crucial to formulate clear and precise queries. For example, instead of asking "Do I need an umbrella today?", it's best to specify the location and even include the date, such as "Will I need an umbrella in Los Angeles tomorrow?" Providing specific details grants Siri more context to understand the intention of the query accurately.

5. Adaptability to Accents and Languages:

Siri boasts an impressive multi-language support system. However, heavy accents or dialects might sometimes be an obstacle for Siri to accurately grasp user commands. Apple has dedicated resources to improving Siri's recognition capabilities across regional accents, but more work can still be done. Patience and practice are key in refining voice recognition, especially for users with unique speech patterns or uncommon languages.

6. Continuous Learning:

Leveraging machine learning and artificial intelligence, Apple is continuously working on enhancing Siri's comprehension abilities. Siri uses data gathered from anonymized user interactions to refine its understanding of various commands or user patterns. Engaging with Siri often can provide valuable data for the system to improve its recognition and interpretation skills. Whenever Siri misunderstands a command, instead of just moving on, trying alternative phrasing or enunciating more clearly can significantly contribute to Siri's learning process.

7. Error Corrections:

If Siri misinterprets your command or provides an inaccurate response, it's recommended to correct it immediately. Simply responding with the right information or rephrasing your command politely can help Siri perform better and reduce future errors. Remember, Siri values user interaction and aims to adapt to individual needs, so your effort in offering corrections can lead to a satisfactory user experience.

8. Utilize Siri Suggestions:

Siri Suggestions are proactive recommendations that Siri provides based on your device usage patterns. They appear in various contexts, such as the lock screen, search, or Siri app suggestions. Siri adapts these suggestions based on your routine, frequently visited places, and often-used apps. Embracing these suggestions not only boosts Siri's comprehension but also helps you discover ways to use Siri to its fullest potential.

In conclusion, Siri's recognition and understanding have significantly evolved over the years, shaping it into a powerful virtual assistant. Nevertheless, there are ways for users to contribute to its continuous improvement. By focusing on clear pronunciation, offering context, enriching vocabulary, providing accurate queries, accommodating diverse accents, engaging in continuous learning, offering error corrections, and utilizing Siri Suggestions, users can optimize Siri's performance, leading to a seamless and enriching user experience.

# 9.3 Troubleshooting Connectivity and Performance Problems

Troubleshooting Connectivity and Performance Problems with Siri

Apple Siri is a powerful digital assistant designed to make our lives easier by performing various tasks through voice commands. However, like any other technology, Siri can occasionally encounter connectivity and performance problems that may hinder its functionality. Inside this guide, we will explore common troubleshooting techniques to help you overcome these issues and ensure a seamless Siri experience.

1. Check your internet connection:

Siri requires an active internet connection to function properly. Start by verifying that your device is connected to a reliable Wi-Fi or cellular data network. If you're experiencing issues with Siri, try the following steps:

a. Toggle Wi-Fi/Cellular Data: Go to your device's settings and turn off Wi-Fi or cellular data for a few seconds, then turn it back on.

b. Reset Network Settings: Under settings, select "General" and then "Reset. " Choose "Reset Network Settings," but be aware that this will erase all of your saved Wi-Fi passwords.

c. Test speed and connectivity: Use a web browser or another internet-dependent app to ensure that your network is functioning correctly. Poor network speed or connectivity may impact Siri's performance.

2. Ensure Siri is enabled:

Sometimes, Siri may appear inactive or non-responsive due to configuration issues. Ensure that Siri is enabled and properly configured:

a. Check Siri settings: Open the Settings app and navigate to "Siri & Search. " Make sure the toggle switch for Siri is turned on. Additionally, check that Siri is enabled for Lock Screen, Home Button/Touch ID, or Side Button depending on your device model.

b. Check language and region settings: Siri may have language and region limitations. Ensure that you have selected the correct language and region preferences for Siri to work optimally.

3. Restart your device:

Restarting your device can effectively resolve various issues. To restart your iPhone or iPad:

a. Hold the power button: Press and hold the power button until the "Slide to power off" slider appears.

b. Power off: Slide the slider to power off your device.

c. Power on: After a few seconds, press the power button again to switch on your device.

4. Update iOS:

Keeping your device's operating system up to date is crucial for optimal Siri performance. To update your iOS:

a. Go to Settings: Open the Settings app on your device.

b. Choose "General": Scroll down and select "General" from the list.

c. Software Update: Tap on "Software Update" and follow the instructions to update your iOS if an update is available.

5. Enhance Siri performance:

If connectivity doesn't seem to be the issue, and Siri is still performing poorly, there are a few tips that may help improve its performance:

a. Clear microphone/access points: Ensure that the microphone ports are free from debris, such as dust or lint, by gently cleaning them with a soft cloth. Additionally, verify that the microphones are not blocked by a case or your hand while speaking to Siri.

b. Disable Low Power Mode: Siri's performance may be restricted in Low Power Mode, as it conserves battery life. Disable Low Power Mode by going to Settings > Battery and turning off the toggle.

c. Reduce background processes: Close unnecessary apps running in the background to give Siri more processing power to prioritize its tasks. Swipe up from the bottom of the screen (or double-click the home button) to view the app switcher, then swipe the app windows off the screen to close them.

Conclusion:

Apple Siri is a remarkable digital assistant, helping users accomplish tasks quickly and efficiently through voice commands. When encountering connectivity and performance issues, it is crucial to troubleshoot and resolve these problems to ensure optimal functionality. By following the steps outlined in this guide, you can diagnose and address common issues, ultimately enhancing your Siri experience and maximizing its potential. Remember, with a stable internet connection, proper device configuration, and regular updates, Siri will reliably assist you in your day-to-day activities.

# Chapter 10: Siri Across Devices

A midst the details of this chapter, we will delve into the capabilities of Apple Siri across various devices. Siri, Apple's virtual assistant, is integrated into several Apple products, including iPhone, iPad, Apple Watch, Mac, and Apple TV. Understanding how Siri operates across these platforms is essential to maximizing its potential and enjoying a seamless experience. Let's explore the amazing functionalities of Siri across devices and learn how to utilize them effectively.

1. Continuity and Handoff:

One of the most impressive features of Siri is its ability to seamlessly transfer tasks across different Apple devices. With Continuity and Handoff, you can start an interaction with Siri on one device and continue it on another. For example, if you start a conversation with Siri on your iPhone, you can pick up right where you left off on your Mac without any interruption. This enables a cohesive Siri experience, enabling you to effortlessly switch devices while keeping your progress intact.

2. Siri on iPhone and iPad:

Siri on iPhone and iPad serves as a convenient personal assistant, helping you with a wide range of tasks. From setting reminders and alarms to sending messages and making phone calls, Siri can handle it all. Moreover, Siri can provide information about weather, sports scores, calculations, translations, and much more. The hands-free capabilities of Siri on these devices allow you to interact with it using just your voice, enabling a hands-free, multitasking experience like never before.

3. Siri on Apple Watch:

On your Apple Watch, Siri becomes an invaluable asset for quick assistance and enhancing your wearable experience. Thanks to its integration with Apple's ecosystem, Siri on Apple Watch provides a swift way to display notifications, check your calendar, or launch apps directly from your wrist. You can easily initiate Siri by raising your wrist, using the "Hey Siri" command, or pressing and holding the Digital Crown button. Siri on Apple Watch is designed for on-the-go convenience and efficiency, making daily interactions hassle-free.

4. Siri on Mac:

Siri integration within macOS makes it effortless to access Siri on your Mac. Whether you are working, researching, or simply browsing the web, Siri can help perform tasks faster and more efficiently. Siri on Mac responds to both voice interactions and on-screen inputs, making it versatile for various user preferences. You can manage files, search the web, control system settings, ask for computational queries, and even interact with third-party apps using Siri on Mac.

5. Siri on Apple TV:

Siri capability on Apple TV redefines entertainment by allowing you to control your television hands-free. Harnessing the power of Siri, you can navigate through apps, search for movies and TV shows, adjust playback controls, and even control home automation tasks using HomeKit-compatible devices. By using your voice, you can swiftly find the content you are looking for and make your entertainment experience more immersive and convenient.

Conclusion:

Apple Siri spreads its wings across multiple Apple devices, providing users with a powerful and consistent virtual assistant experience. From the personalized iPhone and iPad encounters to the convenience of Siri on your Apple Watch, Mac, and Apple TV, Siri can simplify your daily tasks and significantly enhance your digital interactions. These robust and multifunctional capabilities allow users to leverage the power of voice and seamlessly move between devices. Understanding how Siri operates across platforms is instrumental in fully appreciating and benefiting from Apple's virtual assistant. So, make the most of Siri across devices, simplify your routine, and dive into the future of convenient and intelligent voice technology.

# 10.1 Using Siri on Different Apple Devices

U sing Siri on Different Apple Devices
Siri, the virtual voice assistant developed by Apple, has become an integral part of their devices, providing users with a convenient and efficient way to interact with their iPhones, iPads, Macs, Apple Watches, and Apple TVs. Within these chapter, we will delve into how to use Siri on different Apple devices and explore the unique features and capabilities that each device offers.

10.1.1 iPhones and iPads

When it comes to iPhones and iPads, Siri is easily accessible by pressing and holding the home button or the side button, depending on the device model. Alternatively, you can simply say "Hey Siri" if you have enabled this feature in your device settings. Siri will then spring to life and await your command.

On iPhones and iPads, Siri can perform a vast array of functions, ranging from making phone calls and sending text messages to setting reminders and even launching apps. For example, if you want to send a message, you can say "Hey Siri, send a text message to John saying I'll be there in 10 minutes." Siri will transcribe your message and send it on your behalf. Furthermore, Siri can provide information about the weather, sports scores, and even perform basic calculations.

One exciting feature exclusively available on iPhones is Siri Shortcuts. It allows you to create personalized shortcuts for Siri to execute a series of tasks with just a single command. For instance, you can create a shortcut called "Workout Time" that prompts Siri to open your preferred fitness app, play your workout playlist, and set a timer for 30 minutes.

10.1.2 Macs

If you own a Mac, Siri can be accessed by clicking on the Siri icon in the menu bar or by using the keyboard shortcut Command + Space. Once summoned, Siri will eagerly await your queries and commands.

On Macs, Siri can tackle numerous tasks, including searching the web, opening applications, composing emails, and even adjusting system settings.

For instance, you can say "Hey Siri, show me pictures of the Golden Gate Bridge" to quickly browse through beautiful images across the web without launching a browser.

One notable feature unique to Macs is Siri's integration with the Finder app. You can utilize Siri's intelligence to search for files and folders on your computer using natural language commands. For example, saying "Hey Siri, show me all the documents I worked on last week" will prompt Siri to display the relevant files, making it a breeze to locate your recent work.

### 10.1.3 Apple Watches

Apple Watches offer a truly seamless and hands-free experience with Siri as they remain constantly strapped to your wrist. To activate Siri on an Apple Watch, simply raise your wrist and say "Hey Siri," or press and hold the Digital Crown button. Siri on Apple Watches can respond to commands, verbalize information, and even display certain visual content.

With your Apple Watch and Siri, you can set reminders, make phone calls, send messages, initiate workouts, and ask for weather updates. For frequent travelers, you can ask Siri for the current time in different time zones or inquire about currency conversions, making it amazingly convenient when you're globetrotting.

Apple Watches also leverage Siri's proactive approach to keep you informed throughout the day. For example, Siri can display upcoming events from your calendar, provide directions to your next destination, and even suggest apps to launch based on your usage patterns. It's like having a personal assistant right on your wrist.

### 10.1.4 Apple TVs

Apple TV brings Siri to your living room, allowing you to control your entertainment system effortlessly. To summon Siri on Apple TV, simply press and hold the Siri button on the Apple TV remote or activate Siri through the Apple TV app on iPhones, iPads, or Apple Watches.

Siri on Apple TV allows you to browse and stream content, such as movies, TV shows, or even specific genres, just by speaking. You can say "Hey Siri, show me action films" or "Watch the latest episode of Game of Thrones," and Siri will showcase the available options for your viewing pleasure.

What's more, Siri can help you adjust settings on your Apple TV, including volume control or switching between different input sources, provided that your TV is compatible. With Siri, you can effortlessly navigate through app interfaces or seek out specific information about the content you're consuming.

In conclusion, Siri serves as an ever-present digital assistant across multiple Apple devices, each offering unique features and capabilities. Whether you're using Siri on your iPhone, iPad, Mac, Apple Watch, or Apple TV, you can rely on its hands-free convenience, personalized shortcuts, proactive suggestions, and intuitive search capabilities. Let Siri simplify your everyday tasks and enhance your overall Apple device experience.

# 10.2 Syncing Siri Data and Preferences Across Devices

One of the many advantages of using Apple Siri is its ability to sync data and preferences across multiple devices seamlessly. This feature allows you to have a consistent Siri experience regardless of whether you are using Siri on your iPhone, iPad, or Mac.

To get started with syncing Siri data and preferences, ensure that your devices are signed in with the same Apple ID. This is important as Apple ID acts as a unique identifier for your account and enables Siri to link all your devices together. Once you've signed in, follow these steps to sync Siri data and preferences across your devices:

Step 1: Enable iCloud Settings

To begin syncing Siri data, go to the "Settings" app on your iOS device. If you're using a Mac, head to the "System Preferences" and click on "iCloud". In either case, make sure that iCloud is enabled and that Siri is allowed to use iCloud to sync data. This step ensures that your Siri preferences, contacts, reminders, and other relevant data are securely backed up and shared across all your devices.

Step 2: Siri & Search Settings

On your iOS device, navigate to "Settings" and locate the "Siri & Search" option. Tap on it, and you will find various options like "Listen for 'Hey Siri,'" "Language," "Voice Feedback," and more. Customize these settings according to your preferences. For example, enabling "Listen for 'Hey Siri'" allows you to activate Siri by just uttering those words. By default, Apple configures these settings across devices in the same way, providing uniformity.

Step 3: Dictation Language

If you use Siri dictation (speech-to-text feature) frequently, it's crucial to set up the dictation language according to your preferred language. To adjust this setting, follow the same steps mentioned above and choose the preferred language for dictation. Selecting a single language across your devices ensures that Siri understands your voice commands accurately, leading to more precise responses and a better overall experience.

Step 4: Siri Suggestions and Shortcuts

Siri Suggestions and Shortcuts enhance your Siri experience by offering smart suggestions based on your daily habits and preferences. This could include suggesting actions or displaying relevant information based on your app usage patterns. To customize how Siri suggests and interacts with various apps, navigate to "Settings", select "Siri & Search", and browse through the suggested apps and available shortcuts. Tailor these suggestions according to your liking to streamline your Siri usage across devices.

Step 5: Accessibility Settings

Apple always considers accessibility as a crucial aspect of its software and services. Siri, being a central part of the Apple ecosystem, is no exception. For users with specific accessibility needs, Siri offers an array of options. In the "Settings" app, search for and select "Accessibility" and choose the "Siri" option. Here, you can set up features like Type to Siri or Voice Control, allowing you to control Siri using text input or vocal commands, respectively. These settings will be carried over to all your synced devices, ensuring consistent accessibility experience.

Step 6: Customized Siri Responses

When conversing with Siri, sometimes a question or prompt may result in an unexpected response. Fortunately, Apple allows you to tweak Siri's understanding and response to particular custom requests. To teach Siri your preferences and adjust its context-based responses, start a dialogue with Siri and provide feedback. Based on your feedback, Siri will adapt, leading to more tailored interactions in the future. This learning happens on an individual device basis but doesn't affect the overall syncing process.

By following these steps, you will have successfully synced Siri data and preferences across all your compatible devices. From that point forward, any modifications you make to your Siri settings or preferences on one device will be automatically replicated across all devices connected with your Apple ID.

Furthermore, with Siri's flawless synchronization, you can freely switch between your iPhone, iPad, and Mac, knowing that Siri understands your context, preferences, and data across all devices. Whether you need to set reminders, ask for directions, send messages, or even make calls, Siri will be your ever-reliable assistant, well-versed in all your settings, shortcuts, and information, regardless of the device you're using.

Syncing Siri data and preferences provides a seamless and consistent Siri experience, transforming Siri from a device-centric assistant to an intuitive and adaptable companion throughout your Apple ecosystem. So take a moment to sync your Siri data today, and open up a world of intelligent and personalized voice-based features across your Apple devices.

# 10.3 Interactions with Siri on HomePod, Mac, and Apple Watch

Interactions with Siri on HomePod, Mac, and Apple Watch

With the advancement of technology, virtual assistants have become an integral part of our daily lives. Among them, Apple Siri stands out as one of the most popular and widely used personal voice assistants. Siri can be accessed not only on your iPhone and iPad but also on other Apple devices such as HomePod, Mac, and Apple Watch. Enclosed within this chapter, we will explore the various interactions you can have with Siri on these devices, providing you with a comprehensive understanding of how to use it effectively.

1. Interactions with Siri on HomePod:

1. 1 Setting up Siri on HomePod:

Before you can begin interacting with Siri on your HomePod, it is important to set it up correctly. This involves connecting your HomePod to your Wi-Fi network, linking it to your Apple ID, and enabling Siri on it. We'll provide step-by-step instructions on how to achieve this to ensure a smooth setup process.

1. 2 Basic voice commands:

Once Siri is set up on your HomePod, you can start engaging with it using basic voice commands. From asking Siri to play your favorite music or controlling the smart devices in your home, to setting timers and reminders, we will cover a range of useful interactions that make HomePod a convenient and hands-free tool for everyday tasks.

1. 3 Music control and streaming:

As an AI voice assistant, Siri can truly enhance your music listening experience on HomePod. You can ask Siri to play specific songs, artists, or genres, create personalized playlists, and control playback using simple voice commands. Additionally, we'll explore ways to leverage HomePods with multiple users, so everyone can enjoy their own music library through Siri.

2. Interactions with Siri on Mac:

2. 1 Siri setup and activation:

Similar to HomePod, Siri needs to be enabled on your Mac to take full advantage of its capabilities. We will walk you through the process of activating Siri on your Mac and customizing its settings to suit your preferences.

2. 2 System commands and assistance:

Siri can act as a virtual assistant on your Mac, helping you with a wide range of system commands and tasks. We'll delve into how you can use Siri to open applications, search for files, adjust settings, set up meetings and appointments, and even perform calculations quickly and efficiently.

2. 3 Utilizing Siri in hands-free mode:

With the integration of "Hey Siri" functionality, controlling your Mac without physical input becomes a breeze. We will demonstrate how you can enable hands-free mode, allowing you to activate Siri by just speaking the phrase "Hey Siri," and how this feature can significantly enhance your productivity and convenience.

3. Interactions with Siri on Apple Watch:

3. 1 Siri configuration on Apple Watch:

To start interacting with Siri on your Apple Watch, you need to set it up and ensure it is connected with your iPhone. We'll guide you through the configuration process, including how to enable Siri using your voice or by raising your wrist conveniently.

3. 2 Voice commands for notifications and messages:

Siri on Apple Watch offers a seamless way to receive notifications and messages without taking out your iPhone. We'll cover how to utilize Siri to read your messages aloud, dictate replies, send messages to your contacts, and even initiate phone calls, all through simple voice commands on your wrist.

3. 3 Fitness tracking and health assistance:

Beyond basic tasks, Siri on Apple Watch can act as your personal fitness companion. We will explain how you can ask Siri about your daily activity progress, monitor your workouts, initiate fitness challenges, and inquire about your heart rate and other health-related data, facilitating a healthier lifestyle.

Conclusion:

Interacting with Apple Siri on HomePod, Mac, and Apple Watch opens up a world of seamless virtual assistance and convenience in various aspects of your life. Whether it's controlling your home, playing music, managing your tasks, or staying fit, Siri empowers you to perform a myriad of actions with just your voice commands. By following the guidelines and tips presented in this chapter, you'll gain the knowledge necessary to maximize your experience with Siri across multiple Apple devices, making your life more efficient, enjoyable, and interconnected than ever before.

# Chapter 11: Exploring Siri's Future

In Chapter 11, we will take a dive into the exciting world of Siri's future. As Siri continues to evolve and grow in functionality, we can expect even more exciting prospects on the horizon. Amidst the details of this chapter, we will explore some of the potential advancements and upcoming features that may enhance your Siri experience.

1. Voice-based UI Improvements:

One area of significant development in Siri's future lies in improving the voice-based user interface. Apple continually invests in research and development to refine and enhance Siri's natural language processing capabilities. As a result, you can expect Siri to become even better at understanding complex commands, accents, and context-specific queries. Siri will continue to improve its accuracy, making conversing with your device more seamless than ever.

2. Enhanced Natural Language Understanding:

As Siri evolves, Apple aims to make it more conversational and better at understanding the context of your queries. Siri's future will likely see significant improvements in its ability to interpret pronouns and maintain contextual knowledge throughout a conversation. This means that you will be able to ask follow-up questions or refer back to previous inquiries without having to repeat all the necessary details. The goal is to create a more fluid and human-like interaction with Siri.

3. Deep Learning and Context Awareness:

Another exciting area of development is Siri's integration with deep learning techniques and context awareness. Imagine Siri becoming even smarter and more intuitive, anticipating your needs based on your usage patterns, location, calendar, and other contextual parameters. Siri's future may involve proactively suggesting actions, offering reminders, or providing recommendations even before you ask. As Siri continually learns and adapts to your preferences and behavior, it has the potential to become an indispensable virtual assistant.

4. Integration with Third-party Apps and Smart Devices:

Siri's future also holds promise when it comes to wider integration with third-party apps and smart home devices. Currently, Siri supports certain categories of apps and smart home devices but imagine a Siri that seamlessly interacts with a broader range of applications and devices. This could allow you to perform more complex tasks, such as controlling multiple smart devices simultaneously or ordering food from your favorite restaurant directly through Siri.

5. Enhanced Multilingual Support:

As Siri becomes a truly global virtual assistant, Apple understands the importance of enhancing multilingual support. Siri's future will likely involve further language additions, allowing people from various regions across the world to interact with their devices in their native language. It may also include improvements in understanding regional accents and dialects to provide a localized and personalized experience to users worldwide.

6. Privacy and Security Enhancements:

Amidst the details of this age of constant connectivity, privacy and security are understandably significant concerns. Apple prioritizes protecting user data and ensuring that Siri remains a trusted assistant. As Siri's functionalities expand, you can expect Apple to enhance its privacy measures further. Siri's future may involve features like on-device language processing, which means that fewer interactions with Siri would require sending data to Apple's servers, ensuring greater privacy.

Conclusion:

Siri's future holds immense promise, thanks to the relentless efforts of Apple's engineers and developers. With continuous advancements in natural language processing, deep learning techniques, integration with third-party apps, and focus on privacy and security, Siri is primed to become an even more powerful and indispensable virtual assistant. The enhancements discussed in this chapter are just the tip of the iceberg, and we can eagerly anticipate more exciting developments and features in store for Siri users. As Siri's capabilities evolve, your device's ability to assist and simplify various aspects of your life will only continue to grow.

# 11.1 Current Trends in Voice Assistants

In recent years, voice assistants have emerged as one of the most popular and rapidly evolving technologies. With their ability to understand and respond to human commands and queries, voice assistants have become an indispensable part of our lives. Among the many voice assistants available today, Apple Siri stands out as one of the most advanced and user-friendly options. Among these chapter, we will explore the current trends in voice assistants, with a specific focus on Apple Siri. We will delve into the advancements made in natural language processing, machine learning, and contextual understanding that have contributed to the development of more sophisticated voice assistants.

1. Increased Usage and Integration

Voice assistants have witnessed a significant rise in popularity due to their seamless integration with our daily activities. They have become an integral part of smartphones, smart speakers, wearable devices, and even home automation systems. The convenience of hands-free interaction and the ability to control several devices with a simple command have driven the widespread adoption of voice assistants. Siri, being present on Apple devices, including iPhones, iPads, Macs, and Apple Watches, has become deeply ingrained in the Apple ecosystem, providing a consistent and unified user experience.

2. Multilingual Support

As the global appeal of voice assistants continues to grow, multilingual support has become crucial. Users now expect their voice assistants to understand and respond in their preferred language. Smart voice assistants like Siri have made tremendous progress in this aspect, offering support for multiple languages and dialects. For instance, Siri now supports several major languages such as English, Spanish, German, French, Chinese, and Japanese, among others. This trend towards multilingual capability has enabled more inclusive and personalized voice assistant experiences.

3. Improved Natural Language Understanding

One of the most critical areas of development in voice assistants is natural language understanding (NLU). Earlier iterations of voice assistants struggled with accurately interpreting user commands, resulting in frustrating experiences. However, recent advancements in NLU have made voice assistants like Siri more intuitive and capable of comprehending complex queries. Siri can recognize context and subtle nuances in speech to provide more accurate responses. This advancement has enhanced user satisfaction and increased the usefulness of voice assistants in various applications, from general inquiries to controlling smart home devices.

4. Enhanced Context Awareness

Adding contextual awareness to voice assistants has been a significant trend in recent years. Rather than treating each user request as an isolated command, advanced voice assistants like Siri aim to understand and remember the context of past interactions. This allows Siri to provide more tailored and personalized responses. For example, if you ask Siri to set a reminder about buying groceries, later on, when you ask, "What's on my to-do list?", Siri will comprehend that you are referring to the reminder you set earlier. This context preservation has substantially improved the user experience of voice assistants, making them more human-like and efficient.

5. Integration with Third-Party Apps

To expand their functionality and provide users with a wider range of options, voice assistants are increasingly integrating with third-party applications. Siri, on Apple devices, has taken significant steps in this area by opening up SiriKit for developers. SiriKit allows developers to integrate their apps with Siri, enabling users to control and access specific app features using voice commands. This inclusivity has opened doors for endless possibilities, making Siri not only efficient but also versatile.

6. Advancement in Voice Technology

Behind the scenes, voice assistants like Siri leverage cutting-edge technologies to offer seamless experiences. Among these advancements, machine learning and automatic speech recognition (ASR) play pivotal roles. Machine learning algorithms enable voice assistants to learn from user interactions, improving their understanding, responses, and accuracy over time. ASR technology allows Siri to accurately convert spoken words into text, the foundation of a robust voice assistant system. These advancements in voice technology have revolutionized human-computer interactions, allowing for more natural and conversational experiences.

In conclusion, voice assistants have rapidly evolved in recent years, bringing with them a multitude of benefits and conveniences. Apple Siri, in particular, has embraced these advancements and continues to be at the forefront of voice assistant technologies. With increased usage and integration, multilingual support, improved natural language understanding, enhanced context awareness, third-party app integration, and advancements in voice technology, Siri has become an indispensable tool in the Apple ecosystem. As voice assistant technology continues to progress, the future promises even more exciting developments for Siri and its counterparts.

# 11.2 Predictions for Siri's Future Features

As we delve into the world of Apple Siri, it's crucial to recognize that technology is ever-evolving. With relentless innovation and vast amounts of research and development, we can anticipate exciting future features for Siri that will undoubtedly enhance our daily lives. Among this section, we will explore some predictions for Siri's future and the potential capabilities it might possess.

1. Enhanced Contextual Understanding: In the future, Siri will likely have a more profound understanding of context, allowing it to interpret complex queries and provide more accurate and relevant responses. Through improved natural language processing and advanced machine learning algorithms, Siri will learn to grasp the deeper meaning behind user questions, leading to more insightful and personalized interactions.

2. Multilingual Support: Siri currently supports multiple languages, but we can foresee expanded language options. As Apple aims to cater to an increasingly global user base, Siri may evolve to offer support for lesser-known languages or dialects, broadening its reach and accessibility across different cultures and regions.

3. Improved Third-Party Integration: Siri's integration with third-party apps and services has grown significantly in recent years. Going forward, we can expect even deeper partnerships and a wider range of capabilities with various developers. This means Siri could seamlessly interact with apps to schedule appointments, order food, book tickets, control smart home devices, and perform numerous other tasks, all through voice commands.

4. Deeper Web Knowledge: Siri already provides answers to a variety of queries, thanks to its understanding of structured data. However, in the future, Siri might tap into the unstructured wealth of information on the internet. By utilizing advanced web scraping techniques and applying intelligent algorithms, Siri could offer responses that are not limited solely to

pre-determined databases, enabling users to access a vast pool of knowledge at their fingertips.

5. Advanced Emotional Intelligence: Natural language understanding is key to Siri's success, and future advancements may focus on imbuing Siri with emotional intelligence. Siri might be capable of recognizing and responding to emotions in users' voices, adapting its tone and approach accordingly. This human-like interaction will effectively bridge the gap between humans and machines, making Siri feel even more like a personal assistant.

6. Expanded Accessibility: Siri has already made significant strides in aiding individuals with special needs by integrating with accessibility features like VoiceOver. Looking forward, Siri might become an indispensable tool for people with various disabilities, offering increased assistance and support through voice-controlled technology. This could involve helping users manage their daily routines, providing navigation guidance, or even assisting in emergency situations.

7. Proactive Intelligence: In its current iteration, Siri largely responds to user-initiated queries. In the future, Siri may become more proactive by actively monitoring our behaviors, taking note of our preferences, and anticipating our needs. By analyzing user patterns, Siri could predict what tasks we may need assistance with and offer suggestions or reminders to streamline our lives and improve overall efficiency.

8. Increased Hardware Integration: Siri's integration with Apple's hardware ecosystem is continuously expanding. As the range of Apple devices and accessories grow, we can anticipate Siri becoming more intertwined with day-to-day activities. For example, Siri might integrate with future Apple wearables to provide real-time health data, heart rate analysis, or personalized exercise recommendations, leveraging the immense potential of the Internet of Things.

9. Smarter Integration with macOS: Siri on macOS has already proven to be useful, but future iterations might bring even smarter integration with the operating system. Siri may evolve to execute complex tasks like file management, application automation, or efficient multitasking methods, providing both simplicity and speed in our interactions with the macOS environment.

10. Enhanced Privacy Control: Apple has always placed a strong emphasis on user privacy and security. With future advancements, Siri will likely allow users to exercise even more precise control over their personal information. Enhanced privacy features might include the ability to specify the duration for which Siri stores voice recordings, greater granularity in managing third-party app access permissions, and heightened data encryption and anonymization methods.

While these predictions give us an exciting glimpse into Siri's potential future features, it's essential to remember that the field of artificial intelligence is constantly evolving. Apple's commitment to innovation and enhancing user experiences, combined with breakthroughs in natural language understanding and machine learning, will shape Siri into an ever-improving virtual assistant—elevating the possibilities and transforming the way we interact with technology.

# 11.3 Apple's Roadmap for Siri Development

Apple's Siri has become an integral part of our daily lives, making tasks easier and more convenient than ever before. Surrounded by this chapter, we will dive into Apple's roadmap for Siri development, exploring the evolution of Siri and the exciting enhancements Apple has planned for its popular voice assistant.

Since its introduction in 2011, Siri has continuously been evolving to provide users with an enhanced and seamless voice assistant experience. Apple recognizes the immense potential of Siri and is committed to investing significant resources into its development.

One notable area of Apple's roadmap for Siri lies in the domain of natural language processing (NLP). Apple aims to make Siri even more fluent and conversational, allowing users to interact with the voice assistant in a more natural and intuitive manner. As NLP algorithms improve, Siri's ability to recognize and interpret complex commands and questions will be greatly enhanced, leading to a more human-like interaction.

Apple is also actively working on expanding Siri's language capabilities. Currently, Siri supports several languages, including English, German, French, Spanish, Mandarin, and Arabic, among others. However, Apple's roadmap includes further linguistic advancements by adding support for more regional dialects and languages from around the world. This expansion will enable Siri to cater to a more diverse global user base and make it more inclusive for people everywhere.

Another crucial aspect of Apple's roadmap for Siri development is improving its contextual understanding. Apple wants Siri to understand user queries better and provide more relevant and accurate responses. By analyzing user data, such as location, preferences, and previous interactions, Siri will gain a deeper understanding of the user's needs and preferences. This contextual awareness will significantly enhance the assistant's ability to anticipate user actions and provide personalized recommendations, making it an even more integral part of users' daily lives.

Apple is also investing in enhancing Siri's integration with third-party apps and services. The intention is to provide seamless access to various apps and enable users to perform complex tasks effortlessly. This integration will allow Siri to book reservations, order food, make payments, and perform a multitude of other tasks, all through voice commands. By working closely with developers and providing robust APIs, Apple aims to create a vibrant ecosystem of Siri-enabled apps that leverage the assistant's capabilities extensively.

Additionally, Apple is committed to upholding user privacy and data security while advancing Siri's capabilities. The company emphasizes data anonymization and prioritizes user consent in data processing. The roadmap guarantees that Siri's advancements will continue to respect user privacy and adhere to Apple's stringent privacy standards.

In conclusion, Apple's roadmap for Siri development is an exciting journey aimed at making the voice assistant even more powerful and indispensable. With improvements in natural language processing, linguistic capabilities, contextual understanding, app integration, and privacy measures, Siri is poised to become an unparalleled voice assistant in the industry. Embracing Siri's potential and staying up to date with Apple's exciting developments will undoubtedly open up a world of new possibilities for both beginner and experienced users alike. So, dive in and make the most of the ever-evolving Apple Siri!

# Chapter 12: Conclusion and Final Thoughts

A mong this final chapter, we would like to take a moment to reflect upon everything we have covered throughout this book and provide some concluding thoughts on using Apple Siri as a beginner. We hope that this journey has been enlightening, and that you now feel confident in harnessing the power of Siri to simplify your life and enhance your productivity.

Throughout the previous chapters, we discussed the basics of Siri, covering topics such as enabling Siri, setting up voice recognition, and understanding how Siri interacts with various devices and applications. We also explored how to use Siri for everyday tasks, including making calls, sending messages, scheduling events, and searching for information.

One of the key takeaways we hope you have gained from this book is the versatility of Siri. From creating reminders and setting alarms to providing weather updates and turning on/off smart home devices, Siri has the ability to streamline and automate numerous aspects of your daily routine. By implementing Siri into your life, you are granted a virtual assistant that is ready to help out whenever you need it.

We also delved into more advanced Siri features, such as using Siri Shortcuts, editing Siri's speech, and personalizing Settings for a more tailored user experience. Siri Shortcuts allows you to create custom voice commands for specific actions, giving you even greater control and convenience. By becoming familiar with these advanced features, you can truly harness the full potential of Siri and adapt it to your own unique needs.

As with any new technology, we understand that there may be challenges along the way. Siri relies heavily on voice recognition, and there will be instances where it may not understand or interpret your commands accurately. However, don't be discouraged, as Siri continually learns and improves over time. As you interact more frequently with Siri, it becomes accustomed to your voice and speech patterns, leading to enhanced accuracy and better results.

In conclusion, we believe that Siri has the potential to become an indispensable tool in your everyday life. With its ever-expanding capabilities and integration with a wide range of apps and services, Siri empowers you to be more productive, organized, and efficient. By developing a strong foundation of knowledge and practice, you will be well-equipped to maximize the benefits Siri has to offer.

We hope that this comprehensive guide has provided you with the necessary tools and insights to confidently start your journey with Apple Siri. Remember to experiment and explore the various features Siri offers, as it will continually evolve and adapt to meet your needs. Embrace the convenience and ease-of-use Siri brings to your daily routine, and enjoy the hands-free way of interacting with your digital world.

Thank you for your time and dedication in learning about Siri. Your newfound Siri skills are sure to transform the way you engage with your Apple devices and make your life easier. We wish you all the best in your endeavors with Siri, and may it forever be the helpful assistant by your side.

# 12.1 Recap of Key Siri Features and Functions

Recap of Key Siri Features and Functions

Siri, Apple's highly intelligent and voice-activated virtual assistant, offers a wide range of features and functions to assist you with various everyday tasks. Entailed within this chapter, we will recap some of the key features and functions that Siri offers. From basic commands to advanced capabilities, Siri has evolved to become an indispensable tool for Apple users. So, let's dive into a detailed recap of the key Siri features and functions!

1. Voice Control:

One of the primary features of Siri is its voice-controlled interface, allowing users to interact with their Apple devices simply by speaking. By saying "Hey Siri," you can wake up Siri and give commands, ask questions, or request information. Voice control eliminates the need for typing or navigating through menus manually, making it both convenient and user-friendly.

2. Basic Commands:

Siri excels at executing basic commands, especially for device settings and commonly used apps. For example, you can ask Siri to send a text message, make a phone call, set reminders, create calendar events, and check the weather. These fundamental commands can significantly enhance your productivity by saving valuable time and effort.

3. Dictation and Voice Typing:

Siri's dictation capabilities empower users to speak rather than type messages, emails, or any other form of text input. By tapping on the microphone icon within the keyboard, Siri will listen to your voice and convert it into written text accurately. This feature proves incredibly useful when you need to compose lengthy messages or emails without typing a single word.

4. Intelligent Suggestions:

As you continue to use Siri, it learns from your habits and provides intelligent suggestions based on your preferences. For instance, if you frequently call or message a specific contact during a particular time of day, Siri will offer a convenient shortcut on the lock screen or the Siri suggestions widget for easy access. This feature enhances your overall Siri experience by proactively predicting your needs.

5. Web Search:

Siri leverages the power of the internet to provide users with comprehensive and accurate search results. It fetches information from various sources like Wikipedia, news websites, and other online platforms to answer your questions. You can ask Siri general knowledge questions, solve math problems, look up facts about famous personalities, or even search for recipes or restaurant recommendations in your area.

6. Smart Home Integration:

With the ever-increasing popularity of smart home devices, Siri integrates seamlessly with compatible products, allowing you to control your home automation system via voice commands. Whether it's adjusting the thermostat, turning on the lights, or even locking the doors, Siri serves as a virtual hub for managing your connected smart devices. Check with the manufacturers of your smart home products to ensure compatibility with Siri.

7. Apple Music Playlists and Recommendations:

Whether you're a music aficionado or just looking for some tunes to unwind, Siri excels at bringing the world of music closer to you. Siri can shuffle songs, create personalized playlists, suggest new releases based on your taste, or play music from a particular genre or artist. You can also command Siri to control playback options like skipping tracks, adjusting the volume, or playing music on multiple devices simultaneously.

8. Multilingual Support:

Siri supports multiple languages, enabling users from various linguistic backgrounds to benefit from its services. It seamlessly adapts based on the language settings of your iOS device, making Siri a versatile companion for global users. You can switch between languages on-the-go, ensuring a smooth user experience regardless of your preferred language.

9. Third-Party App Integration:

Apple has opened up Siri to third-party app integration, allowing developers to integrate their applications with Siri's capabilities. This enables users to perform complex functions within a wide range of apps, all through voice commands to Siri. For example, you can order a ride with a ride-sharing app, book a restaurant reservation, or initiate a money transfer through digital wallets – all without opening the respective apps manually.

10. Celebrity Voices and Customization:

Apple offers various options for personalizing your Siri experience. Users can choose from a selection of voices, ranging from different genders and accents, to make Siri sound more appealing or relatable. Furthermore, Apple occasionally releases special celebrity voices, adding a touch of excitement and variety to the overall Siri experience.

It's important to note that this recap covers just a fraction of Siri's capabilities and continuously evolving feature set. As technology progresses and Apple introduces new updates, Siri will undoubtedly become even smarter, more reliable, and deliver an ever-improving user experience.

In the next chapter, we will explore some advanced features and functionalities of Siri, which will provide even further insight into Siri's profound capabilities. So, stay tuned and get ready to unravel the full potential of this exceptional virtual assistant!

# 12.2 Tips for Maximizing Your Siri Experience

**12**. 2 Tips for Maximizing Your Siri Experience
Are you tired of manually performing everyday tasks on your Apple device. Look no further. Apple Siri, your intelligent assistant, is here to make your life easier. Embraced by this chapter, we will explore the various methods to maximize your Siri experience. Get ready to unlock the full potential of Siri and streamline your digital life.

1. Keep Siri up to Date:

To ensure Siri functions optimally, keep your device up to date with the latest iOS version. Regular updates introduce new features and improvements, making Siri more capable with every upgrade.

2. Enable "Hey Siri":

Unlock the automatic listening feature of Siri by enabling "Hey Siri" command. Simply open the Settings app, navigate to Siri & Search, and enable the "Listen for Hey Siri" option. You can now activate Siri by simply uttering this handy phrase, even if your device is locked or across the room.

3. Customize Your Siri Settings:

Personalize your Siri settings to create a tailored experience. Adjust Siri's voice gender, language, and even how it responds to activation. In Siri & Search settings, explore options such as Voice Feedback, My Info, and App Support to fine-tune Siri to your liking.

4. Teach Siri About Yourself:

Help Siri assist you better by teaching it about yourself. Head to Contacts and edit your own contact card to include essential details like your name, address, relationships, and other useful information. Siri will use this information intelligently whenever required.

5. Utilize Siri's Language Fluency:

Did you know Siri can understand and communicate in various languages. If you are bilingual or multilingual, Siri makes language switching effortless.

Specify your preferred languages in Siri settings, allowing you to communicate more comfortably and conveniently.

6. Extend Siri's Knowledge with Built-in Apps:

Siri effortlessly integrates with your device's built-in apps. Utilize Siri's capabilities to compose emails, set reminders, schedule meetings, send text messages, make calls, launch apps, play music, and much more. Explore each app and discover the incredible convenience offered.

7. Explore Siri Suggestions:

Siri diligently learns your patterns, activities, and preferences to provide timely suggestions. Glance at your device's Lock Screen, Search, or Siri App Suggestions to discover helpful shortcuts based on your usage behavior. Leverage these suggestions to enhance your Siri experience, making it a proactive digital assistant.

8. Control Settings and Preferences:

Siri's immense power lies in its ability to intelligently control device settings. Whether it's adjusting Wi-Fi, Bluetooth, brightness, or other settings, Siri readily obeys your commands. Simply instruct Siri to toggle specific settings, saving you time digging through menus.

9. Manage Siri Shortcuts:

Enhance Siri's capabilities by creating personalized shortcuts. Navigate to Siri & Search settings, access the My Shortcuts section, and create shortcuts for tasks you frequently perform. Use personalized phrases to command Siri, adding even more efficiency to your digital workflow.

10. Collaborate with Third-Party Apps:

Siri is not limited to Apple's ecosystem anymore. With Siri Shortcuts, it interacts with countless third-party apps. Always look for compatible app updates and explore their Siri integration options. Engaging in this way opens up a world of possibilities, from ordering food deliveries to controlling your smart home devices conveniently.

11. Fine-tune Siri's Pronunciation:

Siri may occasionally mispronounce names or words. Not to worry – you can teach Siri proper pronunciation with ease. When Siri misreads or mispronounces something, swiftly correct it, and Siri will remember the correct pronunciation for future references.

12. Use Siri Across Your Apple Devices:

Siri is not limited to a single device. You can sync Siri across all your Apple devices, including iPhone, iPad, Mac, and Apple Watch. This synchronization allows cross-device continuity and a truly seamless Siri experience, enabling you to pick up right where you left off.

Conclusion:

Now that you've explored these twelve tips, you have all the ingredients to maximize your Siri experience. Armed with the knowledge of Siri's numerous capabilities, you can transform your interactions with your Apple devices. Record reminders, send texts, play music, control settings, and so much more—all with a simple activation phrase. Let Siri become your trusted digital companion, effortlessly handling tasks and assisting you in every way possible. So go ahead and embrace the power of Siri – your personal assistant of the future.

# 12.3 Embracing the Potential of Voice Assistants in Everyday Life

Embracing the Potential of Voice Assistants in Everyday Life
In the rapidly evolving digital landscape, voice assistants have emerged as a revolutionary technology, transforming the way we interact with our devices. Among these digital companions, Apple Siri stands out as an ingenious virtual assistant that seamlessly integrates with Apple devices, enabling users to carry out tasks and obtain information through natural language voice commands. Siri's features and capabilities have expanded over time, making it an indispensable tool that enhances productivity and convenience in our everyday lives. Embedded within this guide, we will delve into Siri's potential, explore its features, and provide you with easy-to-follow steps to learn and maximize your usage of Siri as a beginner.

Understanding Siri's Capabilities:

Before we fully delve into the possibilities offered by Siri, it is important to have a comprehensive understanding of its capabilities. Siri is capable of performing a multitude of tasks, including setting reminders, making phone calls, sending messages, checking the weather, playing music, and much more. Its conversational interface allows users to interact with a natural language processing system, making the experience intuitive and user-friendly. Siri also has a proactive nature, providing personalized and context-aware suggestions, ensuring that you stay informed and save time.

Getting Started with Siri:

To get started with Siri, ensure that your device is compatible with Siri, which includes iPhones, iPads, Apple Watches, Apple TVs, and Macs. The Siri setup process is one of the simplest procedures that Apple offers, involving enabling Siri in the settings. Once Siri is activated, ensure that your internet connection is stable as Siri relies on an active internet connection to function effectively. Additionally, to benefit from Siri's full potential, it is crucial to keep your device software up-to-date as Siri continuously evolves with each iOS update.

Mastering Siri's Basic Features:

Once basic setup is complete, it's time to explore the fundamental features Siri has to offer. Begin by experimenting with Siri's voice recognition capabilities. Simply activate Siri by using the "Hey Siri" command or holding down the Home button, depending on your device. Speak clearly and concisely, providing specific instructions and questions. Siri's artificial intelligence and natural language processing algorithms will initiate the appropriate tasks or answer your queries promptly.

Optimizing Siri for Enhanced User Experiences:

Understanding Siri's basic functionality is just the beginning; to fully embrace Siri's potential, make use of customization options to optimize your user experience. Take advantage of Siri's ability to adapt to your needs by personalizing their responses and preferences. This can be achieved by training Siri to recognize your voice, thereby enhancing accuracy and providing a more tailored experience. You can do this by completing the voice recognition setup process under the Siri settings on your device. Furthermore, provide Siri with access to your calendars, contacts, and other information sources to maximize its usefulness in executing tasks and retrieving information.

Expanding Siri's Usability:

To truly harness the potential of Siri, explore its extensive integration with various applications and services. Siri supports numerous third-party apps, allowing you to perform a wide range of tasks with a simple voice command. Explore available Siri shortcuts in popular apps like Uber, Spotify, Evernote, and WhatsApp, among others. By configuring custom shortcuts, you can automate specific actions such as ordering a ride, playing a specific song, creating notes, or sending a message to a specific contact. The ability to streamline your interactions with multiple apps using Siri not only saves time but also elevates convenience to new heights.

Going Beyond Productivity:

While Siri proves to be an invaluable tool for productivity, its potential transcends mere task management. Siri can be your source of information, capable of providing answers to complex questions by utilizing the vast knowledge bank of the internet. For example, conducting simple inquiries like

"What's the capital of France. ", or even performing mathematical calculations, Siri has you covered. Moreover, Siri can assist in making reservations, providing recommendations, and even engaging in casual banter, making it a truly versatile companion in your day-to-day life.

Voice Assistants as Part of Future Technologies:

The seamless integration between voice assistants and other emerging technologies paves the way for an exciting future. As AI advancements continue to accelerate, Siri and other virtual assistants are likely to become even more intuitive, proactive, and capable of guiding us through our daily lives. We can expect greater device compatibility, allowing us to incorporate voice control across a wide range of smart devices within our homes, vehicles, and workplaces. Moreover, as our understanding of natural language processing improves, the potential applications and impact of Siri in various fields such as healthcare, education, and customer service increases manifold. Its integration across Apple devices brings a touch of innovation and efficiency to our everyday lives. By understanding Siri's capabilities, optimizing user experiences, exploring its extensive integration, and realizing its impact on future technologies, beginners can truly embrace the transformative nature of Siri. So, unlock the potential of Siri and embrace the power of voice assistants as you navigate through this digital era.

Milton Keynes UK
Ingram Content Group UK Ltd.
UKHW012251290324
440241UK00004B/282

9 798224 202461